Developing Management Skills

EFFECTIVE
COMMUNICATION

David A Whetten
Kim Cameron
Mike Woods

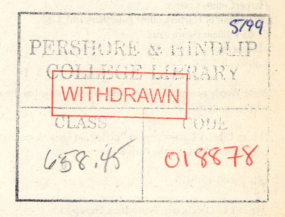

HarperCollins*Publishers*

This edition first published in 1996 by
HarperCollins College
An imprint of HarperCollins Publishers Ltd, UK
77–85 Fulham Palace Road
Hammersmith
London W6 8JB

Mike Woods asserts the moral right to be identified as the author of the
adapted material.

British Library Cataloguing in Publication Data. A catalogue record for this
book is available from the British Library

ISBN 0-00-4990420

Typeset by Dorchester Typesetting Group Ltd
Printed and bound by Scotprint Ltd, Musselburgh
Cover design: The Senate

Other Titles in the Series

Contents

Preface

Effective Communication is one of a series of six books based on *Developing Management Skills for Europe*, a major work by David Whetton, Kim Cameron and Mike Woods. The other titles from this series are *Effective Stress Management, Effective Conflict Management, Effective Empowerment and Delegation, Effective Problem-Solving* and *Effective Motivation*. Presented in a convenient form they provide a background of reading and exercises for tutors and students taking MBA grade or other business qualifications.

Each book in the series seeks to find a balance between a sound theoretical background and relevant case studies. Our objective remains, as it did in the combined work, to develop behavioural skills not only to increase knowledge and understanding in the area, but also to enable readers to apply what they have learned. We hope our readers will be able to achieve their qualifications and become productive members of their organisations by learning applicable skills.

The structure of the books and the method of teaching they employ are, in our opinion, unique. Each book begins with a series of questionnaires designed to check on the reader's present understanding of the area, and in some cases assist the reader in self assessment. Thus, in the present book, *Effective Communication,* the reader is asked to rate his or her ability in communication skills and styles. From these questionnaires, the reader will be able to set learning objectives for the book, and on finishing the text see how much he or she has been able to relate to the very personal world of self.

The main body of the text provides a background to the issues of effective communication, why it is important, and what and how personal communication can be improved. The text closes with case studies, discussion questions, exercises and a section on Application Planning.

Our firm belief is that when 'all is said and done, there is more said than done'. We are asking our readers to make a real commitment to use the material and become more effective in their chosen professions.

Introduction

Over many years of running training courses and workshops, we have asked managers and potential managers to list the skills they most want to acquire. Communication is always included and often at the top of the list. We do not find this surprising since if management is about focusing resources on a task, then communication is the key. People have to be told, sold, coached, consulted, informed and explained to. Information has to be collected, collated and despatched – reports have to be written and meetings held. Communication has to be appropriate – a perfect prose arriving after the event is worthless, but the note on the scrap of paper or the swift and telling phrase, albeit inelegant, maybe exactly what is required.

Not all communication is supportive or needs to be – supportive communication is a two-way process – the speaker is also the listener and the listener can become the speaker. Non-supportive, directive communication has its place – there are times when the job to be done is so confining that there is no time, need or latitude for the communicator to accept feedback. If a child is about to put it's hand in a fire or a walker is about to fall down a hole, that is such a time. The crew of a sinking ship are unlikely to want the opportunity for discussion when the captain is ordering the lifeboats to be manned. However, directive communication can be totally ineffective.

A long time ago when Mike Woods was in a pram, his mother was notified that the postman had been unable to deliver any post 'due to the dog'. She duly attended an interview with a very pompous head postmaster who talked down to her explaining that the refusal by the postman to deliver mail, and run the risk of being bitten by the Woods' household pet, was entirely in the Woods' interest. 'If the postman is bitten, you may well have to pay significant damages.'

He drooled on, in what we call directive communication, not allowing Mrs Woods any comment.

Finally, Mrs Woods had her chance. 'I agree with everything that you say, but there is just one thing that worries me. We do not have a dog.'

The tools of person-to-person communication are obviously words, but in the book *Effective Problem-Solving* we see that words in themselves conjure up images well beyond their literal meaning. Beyond words there lies a complexity of what are called non-verbal signals – for example, who we are or are perceived to be, how we dress, how we gesture – a myriad of complexities that stand between us and clear unequivocal communication.

It may be useful, if the subject of human communication is new to you, to watch your favourite soap opera on TV – for the first half watch it as you would normally and for the second half, turn the sound off and watch only the gestures. The question is, how much did you miss when you could not hear the words? The answer may surprise you.

Skill Pre-assessment

Diagnostic Surveys for Supportive Communication

Communicating Supportively

Instructions
Step 1: Before you read the material in this book, please respond to the following statements by writing a number from the rating scale below in the left-hand column (Pre-assessment). Your answers should reflect your attitudes and behaviour as they are now, not as you would like them to be. Be honest. The instrument is designed to help discover your level of competency in communicating supportively, so you can tailor your learning to your specific needs. The Scoring Key, which will help you to identify the areas of the book most important to you, is at the end of the book (page 73).

Step 2: After you have completed the reading and the exercises in this book, and as many of the Skill Application assignments as possible, cover up your first set of answers. Then respond to the same statements again, this time in the right-hand column (Post-assessment). When you have completed the survey, check out your scores using the Scoring Key at the end of the book (page 73). If your score remains low in specific skill areas, use the behavioural guidelines at the end of the Skill Learning section (page 54) to guide further practice.

Rating Scale

6 Strongly agree	5 Agree	4 Slightly agree
3 Slightly disagree	2 Disagree	1 Strongly disagree

ASSESSMENT

PRE-   POST-

There are times when all of us feel that others are not doing the things that we feel are correct in these situations, and when we feel it is necessary to do something:

1. I understand clearly when it is appropriate to offer advice and direction to others and when it is not.

2. I help others recognise and define their own problems when I counsel them.

3. I am completely honest in the feedback that I give to others, even when it is negative.

4. I always give feedback that is focused on the problem and its solution, not on the characteristics of the person.

5. I always explain the reason for my giving negative feedback with an explanation of what I perceive as having been done wrongly.

6. When I correct someone's behaviour, our relationship is almost always strengthened.

7. I am descriptive in giving negative feedback to others. That is, I objectively describe the event, its consequences and my feelings about it.

8. I always suggest some specific alternatives to those whose behaviour I am trying to correct.

9. I make sure to reinforce other people's sense of self-worth and self-esteem in my communication with them.

10. I convey genuine interest in the other person's point of view, even when I disagree with it.

11. I don't talk down to those who have less power or less information than I do.

12. I convey a sense of flexibility and openness to new information when presenting my point of view, even when I feel strongly about it.

13. I strive to identify some area of agreement in a discussion with someone who has a different point of view.

14. My feedback is always specific and to the point, rather than general or vague.

15. I don't dominate conversations with others.

16. I take responsibility for my statements and point of view by using, for example, 'I have decided' instead of acting as an agent and saying 'they have decided'.

17. When discussing someone's concerns, I use responses that indicate understanding rather than advice.

_____ _____ 18. When asking questions of others in order to better understand their viewpoint, I generally ask 'what' questions instead of 'why' questions.

_____ _____ 19. I hold regular, private, one-to-one meetings with people I work with and/or live with.

_____ _____ 20. I am clear about when I should coach someone and when I should provide counselling instead.

Communication Styles

Instructions

In this questionnaire some managerial experience is assumed. If you do not have such experience assume the role of a good manager and use your imagination.

The questionnaire is divided into two parts:

■ In Part I, four people complain about problems they face in their jobs. Following each complaint are five possible responses. Rank three of the responses you would be most likely to make in reverse order, with 3 being your first choice, 2 being your second choice and 1 being your third choice.

■ Part II describes a particular situation. Several pairs of statements follow. Place a tick next to the one statement in each pair that you would be most likely to use in responding to the given situation. The Scoring Key for this questionnaire can be found at the end of the book (page 73).

Part I

1. 'I've been in this job for six months and I hardly know anyone at all in the company. I just can't seem to make friends or to be accepted by other people. Most people are extremely busy and don't take time to socialise. I feel isolated and excluded from what's going on.'

_____ a. Don't be concerned about not making friends so soon. Things will get better the longer you're with the company.

_____ b. When you first meet people, what do you say? Are you the one to be friendly first?

_____ c. Because company employees are so busy, probably no

one has time to get close socially. You shouldn't expect too much.

_____ d. So you're feeling that people haven't accepted you in the company?

_____ e. It's not as serious as you may feel. When I first joined the company it took me more than six months to get settled in, I still don't know everyone.

2. 'I can't stand my boss. He is the most autocratic, demanding person you can imagine. I've never worked around anyone who cared less for his employees than he does. His complete insensitivity and lack of humanity have made this place miserable.'

_____ a. You sound as if you're having difficulty dealing with rigid control and authority.

_____ b. I know how you feel because last year we had a woman in our department who would drive anybody round the bend. She was the ultimate domineering boss.

_____ c. You're going to have problems unless you work this out. I think you should go to him and tell him how you feel.

_____ d. You really are having a hard time adjusting to your boss, aren't you?

_____ e. Why is it you feel so strongly about him?

3. 'What I want to know is, what happened on that last promotion decision? I thought I was in line for it. I'm sure no one else in the department has my experience, and the whisper I heard indicated the job was mine for the asking. I'm really disappointed that you brought in someone from the outside over me. I don't think it's fair. What does it take to get promoted around here?'

_____ a. What was it that made you think this promotion was yours, George? Are you aware of the requirements of the job and what kind of person we were looking for?

_____ b. Don't be discouraged, George. Your work is good, and if you're patient I'm sure other chances will come along. I'll try to help you be ready next time.

_____ c. I think you have the wrong impression about this,

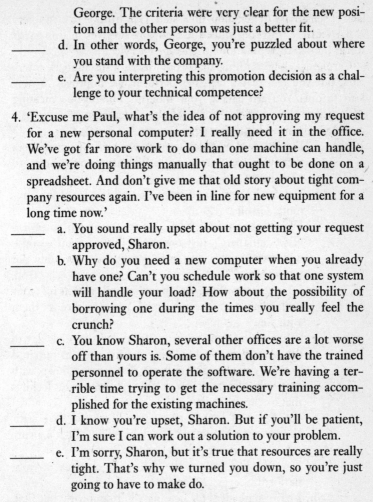

George. The criteria were very clear for the new position and the other person was just a better fit.

_____ d. In other words, George, you're puzzled about where you stand with the company.

_____ e. Are you interpreting this promotion decision as a challenge to your technical competence?

4. 'Excuse me Paul, what's the idea of not approving my request for a new personal computer? I really need it in the office. We've got far more work to do than one machine can handle, and we're doing things manually that ought to be done on a spreadsheet. And don't give me that old story about tight company resources again. I've been in line for new equipment for a long time now.'

_____ a. You sound really upset about not getting your request approved, Sharon.

_____ b. Why do you need a new computer when you already have one? Can't you schedule work so that one system will handle your load? How about the possibility of borrowing one during the times you really feel the crunch?

_____ c. You know Sharon, several other offices are a lot worse off than yours is. Some of them don't have the trained personnel to operate the software. We're having a terrible time trying to get the necessary training accomplished for the existing machines.

_____ d. I know you're upset, Sharon. But if you'll be patient, I'm sure I can work out a solution to your problem.

_____ e. I'm sorry, Sharon, but it's true that resources are really tight. That's why we turned you down, so you're just going to have to make do.

Part II

You are the manager of Carole Thompson, a 58-year-old supervisor with 21 years' service with the company. Carole retires in two years time but her performance is sliding, she will not take on any extra work and the work she does do is often found to be lacking. Her attitude towards customers is often brusque and she shows a lack of sensitivity to her shop–floor staff. Her attitude to customers is particularly worrying since the company survives in this harsh world though its reputation for customer service.

Carole has done nothing that would merit a disciplinary interview, but you feel that unless her performance improves, it may lead to one. You are having your monthly one-on-one meeting with her in your office. Which of the statements in each pair would you be most likely to use?

1. _____ a. I've received complaints from some of your customers that you are not being sufficiently sympathetic to complaints and requests.

_____ b. You don't seem to be motivated to do a good job anymore, Carole.

2. _____ c. I know that you've been doing a great job as supervisor, but there's just one small thing I want to raise with you about a customer complaint – probably not too serious.

_____ d. I have some concerns about several aspects of your performance on the job and I'd like to discuss them with you.

3. _____ e. When one of your subordinates called the other day to complain that you had criticised his work in public, I became concerned. I suggest that you sit down with that subordinate to work through any hard feelings that might still exist.

_____ f. You know, of course, that you're wrong to have criticised your subordinate's work in public. That's a sure way to create antagonism and lower morale.

4. _____ g. I would like to see the following changes in your performance: (1), (2) and (3).

_____ h. I have some ideas for helping you to improve; but first, what do you suggest?

5. _____ i. I must tell you that I'm disappointed in your performance.

_____ j. Several of our employees seem to be unhappy with how you've been performing lately.

Skill Learning

The Importance of Effective Communication

Effective communication is a key skill for all managers and may involve a broad array of activities from writing to speech-making. All these activities are important, but the dominant skill for virtually all is effective face-to-face, one-to-one communication. In a study of 88 organisations, both from the public and private sectors, Crocker (1978) found that, of 31 skills assessed, interpersonal supportive communication skills were rated as the most important. Thorton (1966) summarised a variety of survey results by stating, 'A manager's number-one problem can be summed up in one word: communication.' This is hardly surprising since some 80 per cent of all managers' time is spent on verbal communication.

In a study of major manufacturing organisations undergoing large-scale changes, Cameron (1988) asked two key questions: (1) What is your major problem in trying to get organisational changes implemented? and (2) What is the key factor that explains your past success in effectively managing organisational change? To both questions a large majority of managers gave the same answer – *communication*. They also agreed that it is better to err on the side of too much communication than too little. It would seem surprising, then, that in light of this agreement by managers about its importance, communication remains a major problem for managers. Why is this?

Perhaps the most important reason is that most of us see ourselves as good communicators. We feel that communication problems are caused by other people and not ourselves. Haney (1979) reported on a survey of more than 8,000 people in universities, businesses, military units, government and hospitals, in which virtually everyone felt that he or she was communicating at least as well as and, in many cases, better than almost everyone else in the organisation. Most people readily admit that their organisation is fraught with faulty communication, but it is almost always 'other people' who are responsible. Thus, while most agree that proficiency in interpersonal communication is critical to managerial success, most individuals don't seem to feel a strong need to improve their *own* skill level.

Focus on Accuracy

Much of the writing on interpersonal communication focuses on the accuracy of the information being communicated, and emphasises that the communication skill which needs the greatest improvement is the ability to transmit clear, precise messages. Inaccurate communication can have humorous as well as serious results.

> A motorist in an old car was stopped by the police for a roadside check. Everything seemed fine. The officers decided to test the brakes.
> 'Right, we would like you to drive at about 30 mph in front of our police car and when you hear the sound of our horn, make an emergency stop. Give the brakes everything they have got – OK?'
> The driver did all that was asked of him but unfortunately the 30 mph began to pile up traffic behind and one impatient driver of a sports car forced to overtake vented his anger by shaking his fist and sounding his horn. The old car, the brakes of which were in fact very good, stopped immediately and the police car banged straight into him.
>
> (Source: a student legend of the 1950s used by Richard Gordon in his book, *Doctor in the House.*)

> A woman of 35 came in one day to tell me that she wanted a baby but had been told that she had a certain type of heart disease that, while it might not interfere with a normal life, would be dangerous if she ever had a baby. From her description, I thought at once of mitral stenosis. This condition is characterised by a rather distinctive rumbling murmur near the apex of the heart and especially by a peculiar vibration felt by the examining finger on the patient's chest. The vibration is known as the 'thrill' of mitral stenosis. When this woman had undressed and was lying on my table in her dressing gown, my stethoscope quickly found the heart sounds I had expected.

Dictating to my nurse, I described them carefully. I put my stethoscope aside and felt intently for the typical vibration which may be found in a small and variable area of the left chest. I closed my eyes for better concentration and felt long and carefully for the tremor. I did not find it, and with my hand still on the woman's bare breast, lifting it upward and out of the way, I finally turned to the nurse and said: 'No thrill.' The patient's eyes flashed, and with venom in her voice she said, 'Well, isn't that just too bad! Perhaps it's just as well you don't get one. That isn't what I came for.' My nurse almost choked, and my explanation still seems a nightmare of futile words (Loomis, 1939).

Pizza Hut, in their point of sale advertisements. Include the words – *'Order by phone – if not collected in 20 minutes – £1 off'*. Perhaps they meant – *'Order by phone – if not ready for collecting in 20 minutes we will charge you £1 less than our quoted prices.'*

Attempts to improve the communications of an organisation often centre on improving the *mechanics*: networked phones, fax systems, electronic mail, answering machines and desk top publishing. Sophisticated information-based technology has made major strides in enhancing both the speed and accuracy of communication. There is a snag, however, about any mechanical information processing, and a statement Josiah Stamp made over 80 years ago illustrates this point:

The government are very keen on amassing statistics. They collect them, add them, raise them to the nth power, take the cube root and prepare wonderful diagrams. But you must never forget that every one of these figures comes in the first instance from the village watchman, who just puts down what he pleases.

Stamp might well have said 'garbage in garbage out.'

However, irrespective of the availability of sophisticated information technologies and elaborately developed models of communication processes, individuals still communicate pretty much as they please. They can be ineffectively abrasive, insensitive and plain misguided.

More recently, progress has been made in group communications – team briefings, company newsletters, etc., – but comparable progress has not occurred in the interpersonal aspects of communication. People still become offended at one another, make insulting statements and communicate clumsily. The interpersonal aspects of communication involve the nature of the relationship between the communicators. The effect of who says what to whom, what is said, why it is said, and how it is said on the relationship between people has important implications for the effectiveness of the communication, aside from the accuracy of the statement. The interaction between the message, the messenger and a backlog of suppositions and preconceptions about the messenger and his or her role – collectively called the *shadow* – is discussed by Woods and Whitehead (1993).

Ineffective communication may lead individuals to dislike each other, be offended by each other, lose confidence in each other, refuse to listen to each other and disagree with each other. These interpersonal problems, in turn, generally lead to restricted communication flow, inaccurate messages and misinterpretations of meanings. Figure 1 summarises this process.

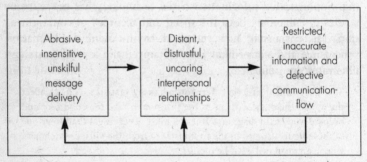

FIGURE 1 Relationships between unskilful communication and interpersonal relationships

To illustrate, consider the following situation.

Alan is involved in setting up an initiative to overcome a quality problem in the final assembly of portable tape recorders.

After Alan's carefully prepared presentation to the management meeting, John raises his hand. 'In my opinion, this is a naive approach to solving our quality problems. It's not as easy as Alan seems to realise. I don't think we should waste our time by pursuing his plan any further.'

John's opinion may be justified, but the manner in which he delivers the message will probably eliminate any hope of its being dealt with objectively. Instead, Alan will probably hear 'You're naive. You're stupid. You're incompetent.' We wouldn't be surprised if Alan's response was defensive or even hostile. Any good feelings between the two have probably been jeopardised and their communication will probably be reduced to self-image protection. The merits of the proposal will be smothered by personal defensiveness. Future communication between the two will probably be minimal.

What is 'Supportive Communication'?

We are focusing on the kind of interpersonal communication that allows managers to communicate accurately and honestly without jeopardising interpersonal relationships. This type of interpersonal communication we will call **supportive communication**. With supportive communication not only is a message delivered accurately, but the relationship between the two communicating parties is supported, even enhanced, by the interchange. Positive interpersonal relationships result. However, the goal of supportive communication is not merely to be liked by other people or to be judged to be a nice person. It is not merely to produce social acceptance but has positive value in organisations. Researchers have found, for example, that organisations that encourage supportive communications enjoy higher productivity, faster problem-solving, improved quality and reduced unproductive conflict, compared with groups and organisations where the communications style is less positive. Moreover, delivering world class customer service is almost impossible without using supportive communication. Effective customer service requires supportive communication skills. Therefore, not only must managers be competent in using this kind of communication, but they must help their subordinates develop this competency as well.

Good employee relations are an essential for any effective organisation (Ouchi, 1981; Peters, 1988). Working with 40 major organisations in America, Hanson (1986) found that over a five-year period, employee relations was by far the most significant factor in their success – more important than the four next most powerful variables (market share, capital availability, firm size and sales growth rate) combined. Techniques that foster good employee relations are not simply a 'feel good factor' that can be abandoned under pressure – they make sound buisness sense. There is however, a strong proviso – some organisational cultures do not accept the concepts of supportive communication.

> A very simple test is recommended. Imagine your boss has asked you to prepare a detailed report on a particular part of your department's work to the Board. One of your subordinates has the skills, knowledge and aptitude for writing the report and you do not. He or she writes the report, which, on your restricted expertise, seems excellent.
>   In your opinion would the organisation expect you to:
> 1. Take the report and present it to the Board.
> 2. Take your subordinate with you to the Board and endorse his or her presentation.
> 3. Sit back while the report is presented.
> 4. Allow the subordinate to present the report, your own presence being irrelevant.

If you feel that 1) or 2) would be 'the way things are done' in your organisation, you may find the whole concept of supportive communication a dangerous concept to pursue.

Coaching, Counselling and Consulting

The principles of supportive communication are probably best introduced by their application to the challenging tasks of coaching, counselling and consulting subordinates (Ross, 1986). They apply to a broader array of managerial communications – negotiation, criticising ones subordinates, peers and bosses and handling conflict. However, coaching, counselling and consulting are almost universal managerial activities with a firm place in the management process.

Hersey and Blanchard (1969 and subsequent editions) can be interpreted as seeing management of subordinates as a sequence:

■ We begin with a high task concern from the manager with a low need for individual relationships with subordinates. The manager needs to know what has to be done and he or she TELLS, in some way, others to do it.

In the ideal state we then move progressively to:

- A high concern for the task coupled with a high concern for individuals. The manager is still in control of the task but needs to be able to make sure that others are able to do it – coaching, and have the aptitude to do it – counselling.
- The task concerns reduce – we know that subordinates have the skills and motivation to do the task but individually need to develop a working procedure with you, the manager – low task and high relationship as Hersey and Blanchard put it. Subordinates are capable and willing in theory to take on the task, but the manager needs to add CONSULTATION as a continuing role of coaching and counselling. As people take over the task, they begin to know more about how they will do it than you, the manager, but you must extend your role for outside communications and monitor the work that is done to ensure that it meets the standards and constraints that are laid down.
- Low task and low relationships. The manager is now able to DELEGATE and part of the job that is delegated is the maintenance of relationships.

The ineffective manager moves from TELLING to DELEGATING without passing through the two high relationship stages, and without using the principle skills of supportive feedback – coaching, counselling and consulting.

- The clarity of the progression is not always obvious in the real world. Coaching and counselling may be needed at any time in management – if only because employees lose motivation or the skills base towards the task changes. Thus, tasks do not *stay* delegated and the effective manager needs to able to act appropriately all the time.
- The progression from TELLING to DELEGATING is not inevitable. The manager may simply not have the time to coach, counsel and consult, the task may be unclear or the organisation may not ALLOW the manager to delegate.

Coaching, counselling and consulting are essentially about the maintenance of relationships and are especially important for the following roles:

- Facilitation – equipping the person for the job and finding training needs.
- Dealing with inappropriate behaviour or attitudes.
- Developing working procedures for the mutual benefit of the individual and all others concerned.
- Appraising and rewarding good performance.
- Correcting poor performance.
- Developing standards and targets.

In this book we will discuss the first three roles, standard setting and appraising will be covered in another book from the present series, *Effective Motivation*, as will be the issues of rewarding and correcting behaviour.

The first question we always need to answer is – what are our objectives in each case – if you do not know where you are going, you will certainly end up somewhere else.

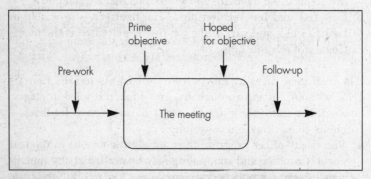

FIGURE 2 Planning for coaching, counselling and consulting meetings

Figure 2 summarises the process. As a manager, faulty human communication can have serious consequences and planning is advisable wherever possible.

Mary managed a floor of telephone sales people in a major financial institution. One of her subordinates, Harry, was noted for leaving early and putting work onto other people. On the afternoon in question she was talking with her floor supervisor when she noticed Harry was putting on his coat and leaving. Confirming on her watch that Harry should still be at his station she called out across the floor:

'Where are you going?'

'Out.'

Mary ran after Harry and narrowly missed hitting the door as Harry slammed it behind him. The loss of face was very difficult for Mary to retrieve.

So planning for any potential problem situation (coaching, counselling and consulting can all give unexpected problems) is advisable. For example:

- **Prework** – what do you need to do BEFORE the meeting?
- **Prime objective** – what do you HAVE to achieve at the meeting?
- **Hoped for objective** – what would you LIKE to get from the meeting?
- **Follow-up** – what needs to be done AFTER the meeting?

Below, we will go through two scenarios which will attempt to answer these four questions. How would you approach the situation so that the problems are solved and, at the same time, your relationships with you subordinates are strengthened? What are the basic problems in these two cases? What would you say, and how would you say it, so that the best possible outcomes resulted? The focus of this book is to help you improve your skills in handling situations such as those detailed below.

Consider the following scenarios:

Tim Nelson is the manager of the division sales force in your firm, which makes and sells components for the aerospace industry. He reports directly to you. Tim's division consistently misses its sales projections, its revenues per salesperson are below the company average, and Tim's monthly reports are almost always late. You make another appointment to visit Tim after getting the latest sales figures, but he isn't in his office when you arrive. His secretary tells you that one of Tim's sales managers has just complained that some employees are arriving late for work and taking extra-long coffee breaks. Tim has immediately gone with the manager to give the salespeople a 'pep talk' and to remind them of performance expectations. You wait for fifteen minutes until he returns.

Betty Mason has an MBA and came highly recommended when she recently joined your firm in the financial planning group. However, she seems to be trying to enhance her own reputation at the expense of others. You have heard increasing complaints lately that Betty is arrogant, self-promotional and openly critical of other group members' work. In your first conversation with her about her performance she denied that there was a problem. She said that, if anything, she was having a positive impact on the group by raising its standards. You arrange another meeting with Betty after the latest set of complaints from her colleagues.

Coaching and Counselling Issues

First, let us distinguish between two basic kinds of interpersonal communication issues faced by managers. Our two case studies above are designed to look at both the **coaching** issues and the **counselling** issues.

Coaching Issues

Coaching issues are those in which managers assist their employees to do their **jobs** effectively – about the task, not about the person.

As Tim's manager, we have to look at our overall objective in meeting him – we would see this objective as something like 'getting him up to speed'. He has, in our opinion, potential but lacks the relevant skills and information. It is a matter for coaching. Issues such as Tim's may be caused by lack of ability, motivation or incompetence but more often they are due to not providing and continuing to provide sufficient accurate, relevant information and training for the subordinate to function effectively. Using the Hersey and Blanchard model, we have a high task and a high relationship concern – the manager needs to maintain a strong concern for the task while helping the subordinate. We would always recommend tackling the coaching issues first, and should the problem remain, look at the more tortuous issues of motivation.

Tim was accepting upward delegation from his subordinates and was not allowing them to solve their own problems. By not insisting that his subordinates bring recommendations for solutions to him instead of problems, and by intervening directly in the problems of his subordinate's subordinates, Tim became overloaded while interfering with his subordinates development. (This issue is dealt with in detail in the book of this series – *Effective Stress Management*) Productivity almost always suffers in cases where one person is trying to resolve all the problems and run the whole show. Tim needs to be coached regarding how to avoid upward delegation and how to effectively delegate responsibility as well as authority.

- **Pre-work** – We would need to check that we had good information before we take action. This is particularly important if we are new to the job.
- **Prime objective** – We believe he is a potentially good worker who needs help. We need to identify what help is needed.
- **Hoped for Objective** – To develop agreed procedures for training and information flow so that Tim can progress and develop.
- **Follow-up** – Monitor that what has been agreed on and implemented, AND monitor Tim's progress.

The Counselling Problem

Counselling problems are about the person doing the task, their suitability, motivation and aptitudes – our example is the Betty Mason case study. As with the coaching issue, the first point to consider is the overall objective. Betty is presenting a serious challenge to the efficient running of the unit. The bottom line is, that should she not accept your advice, you would 'regretfully' be willing to see her go. As a manager there is only a certain amount of quality time available and although employee relations are a significant part of your job, they are rarely factors upon which YOU are judged.

Betty, in the Hersey and Blanchard model, seems to have the task skills to do the job, but the way she is doing it is giving difficulty – the manager needs to keep a low concern for the task and a high concern for relationships.

Managers need to counsel subordinates instead of coach them when the problem stems from attitudes, personality clashes, defensiveness or other factors tied to emotions. Betty's competency or skill is not a problem, but her unwillingness to recognise that a problem exists or that a change is needed on her part requires counselling by the manager. Betty is highly qualified for her position, so coaching or giving advice would not be a useful approach. Instead, an important goal of counselling is to help Betty recognise that a problem exists and to identify ways in which that problem might be addressed. Coaching applies to ability problems, and the manager's approach is 'I can help you do this better'. Counselling applies to attitude problems, and the manager's approach is 'I can help you recognise that a problem exists'.

■ **Pre-work** – We would suspect the meeting could well become acrimonious so we need to feel well in ourselves. We would be advised to understand our organisation's disciplinary procedures, should it come to that, and our own authority. We would also need, as in the Tim case study, to check on our facts.

■ **Prime Objective** – To get Betty to recognise that SHE has a problem to handle. If she refuses to accept that there is any problem we should be prepared to close the meeting and reconsider our actions.

■ **Hoped for Objective** – Betty accepts the need for her to change and we agree some goals – for example, we could recommend the Small Wins Strategy discussed in the *Effective Stress Management* book. We also need to set up an agreed monitoring procedure.

■ **Follow-up** – Monitoring the results of the agreed action, with the option of being flexible in our response if things do not go the way we want.

Of course, many problems involve both coaching and counselling. Frequently managers have to give direction and advice (coaching), as well as help facilitate understanding and willingness to change (counselling). However, the importance of recognising the difference between these two types of problems is that a mismatch of problem with communication approach can aggravate the problem rather than resolve it. For example, to give direction or advice (coaching) in a counselling situation often increases defensiveness or resistance to change. Advising Betty Mason about how to do her job or about the things she should not be doing (such as criticising others' work), for example, will probably only magnify her defensiveness since she doesn't perceive there is a problem. Similarly, counselling in a situation that calls for coaching simply sidesteps the problem and doesn't resolve it. Tim Nelson knows that a problem exists, for example, but he doesn't know how to resolve it. Coaching is needed, not problem recognition. Should you find yourself doing both coaching and counselling in the same interview, we suggest that you adopt some token way of underlining your changing role in the meeting. For instance, should the meeting with Tim go drastically wrong and he begins to attack you and the organisation, it may well be useful to stand-up, go over to a window and sit down again in a different chair. People need to know whether they are talking to a coach, an essential friend, or a counsellor who in this context is a potential threat.

If we accept that the purpose of supportive communication is to produce empowered subordinates, the strategy must be to relinquish as much control as possible to the subordinate.

> In an exercise in employee empowerment, the BP research laboratories in the UK decided to 'trust' their employees and removed all controls from their stores. In principle, and virtually in fact, anyone could take whatever he or she liked without having to consult or fill in any documentation. The legend has it that the stores were empty before the end of the week.

The story illustrates that all stages – telling, coaching, counselling, consulting and delegating need to be followed in sequence. However, they need to be followed in a manner adjusted to the individual's motivation and skill level. Imagine having a subordinate who is a world class expert on database management and attempting to coach them on their own area!

The question that remains, however, is, 'How do I effectively coach or counsel another person?' What are the behavioural guidelines that help me perform effectively in this situation? Both coaching and counselling rely on the same set of key supportive communication principles.

Defensive and Patronising Behaviours

If principles of supportive communication are not followed when coaching, counselling or consulting subordinates, two major problems result that lead to a variety of negative outcomes (Gibb, 1961; Sieburg, 1978). These two major problems are summarised in Table 1.

Table 1   Supportive communication helps overcome defensive behaviour in others and patronising behaviour from ourselves

Defensive behaviour	Patronising behaviour
■ One individual feels threatened or attacked as a result of the communication. ■ Self-protection becomes paramount. ■ Energy is spent on constructing a defence rather than on listening. ■ Aggression, anger, competitiveness, and/or avoidance are common reactions.	■ One individual feels incompetent, unworthy or insignificant as a result of the communication. ■ Attempts to re-establish self-worth take precedence. ■ Energy is spent trying to portray self-importance rather than on listening. ■ Showing off, self-centred behaviour, withdrawal, and/or loss of motivation are common reactions.

If an individual feels threatened or punished by the communication, both the message and the interpersonal relationship is blocked, and one or more of the parties moves into self-protective or defensive behaviour. Criticism perceived as an attack can generate a range of responses – anger, aggression, competitiveness or avoidance – all of which are individual responses designed to defend.

Patronising behaviour occurs when one of the communicating parties feels put down, ineffectual or insignificant because of the communication. Recipients of the communication feel that their self-worth is being questioned, so they focus more on building themselves up rather than listening. Reactions are often self-aggrandising or show-off behaviours, loss of motivation, with-drawal and loss of respect for the offending communicator. Taking the Betty example, we are expecting defensive behaviour from Betty, therefore we need to avoid patronising behaviour in our-selves. In practice, the behaviours may well be quite different. Betty may patronise us for being 'a new manager who will learn in time.' We may then, quite reasonably, become defensive.

In order to overcome these two major problems the eight com-mandments (or principles) of supportive communication need to be followed (see Table 2).

Table 2 The eight commandments of supportive communication

1. **Play the ball and not the player** – supportive communication is about problems and not personalities. 'How can we solve this problem?' NOT 'Because of you there is a problem.'

2. **Establish common ground** – supportive communication begins by establishing a starting point accepted and valued by BOTH parties. 'Our job is to get the product out on time, delays are costing us money.' NOT 'Company profits are down . . .', the poor man might only be responsible for the despatch department.

3. **'Judge not or you will be judged'** – supportive communication is descriptive, not evaluative. 'Here is what happened; here is my reaction; here is what I suggest that would be more acceptable to me.' NOT 'You are wrong for doing what you did.'

4. **Supportive communication should validate rather than invalidate individuals** – don't put people down. 'I have some ideas, what do you think?' NOT 'You wouldn't understand, so we'll do it my way.'

5. **Be specific and not global** – 'You interrupted three times during the meeting.' NOT 'You're always trying to get attention.'

6. **There is a time and a place for everything** – supportive communication needs to be part of a general flow and not something that stands out. 'I agree that we have problems in dispatch. That brings me on to the pallet problem in No. 1.' NOT 'I see you are on the way to the canteen. What are you doing about Max and his sickness record.'

7. **Remember that YOU are paid to do the job** – never delegate upward and never even imply personal disloyalty. 'I cannot approve your request because' NOT 'You have a pretty good idea, but they just wouldn't approve it.'

8. **Supportive communication is not a one-way street** – always be prepared to listen and act on what you hear; never be dismissive. 'I think what you said needs some further discussion, however we have immediate problems today. Let's make a date for the other issues early next week. Is that OK?' NOT 'Fine, I hear what you say but . . .'

The Eight Commandments of Supportive Communication

1. Play the ball and not the player – supportive communication is about problems and not personalities.

Any communication that concentrates on the characteristics of the individual can be interpreted as saying that the person is inadequate. Since we can at least attempt to change what we do, but cannot begin to change what we are, there is nothing we can do about personally directed criticism. The relationship fails and the problems are not solved. Personal criticism is often used to try to persuade the other individual that 'this is how you should feel' or 'this is what kind of person you are' (e.g., 'You are an incompetent manager, a lazy worker or an insensitive colleague'). But since most individuals accept themselves as they are, the common reaction to person-oriented communication is for the recipient to defend him/herself against it or reject it outright. Even when communication is positive (e.g., 'You are a wonderful person'), it may not be viewed as trustworthy if it is not tied to a behaviour or an accomplishment. The absence of some agreed and possible behavioural change is the key weakness in person-oriented communication.

Communication directed towards a specific problem and its solution is useful even when personal appraisals are called for, since they focus on behaviours and events. Statements such as 'You are an autocrat' and 'You are insensitive' are person-oriented, for example, while 'I seldom meet you to help make decisions' and 'Our relationship is deteriorating' are more descriptive of problems. Imputing motives to an individual is person-oriented (e.g., 'It's because you want to control other people'), whereas expressing concern about overt manifestations of behaviour is problem-oriented (e.g., 'You made several sarcastic comments in the meeting today').

In coaching and counselling, problem-oriented communication should also be linked to accepted standards or expectations rather than to personal opinions. Personal opinions are more likely to be interpreted as person-oriented and arouse defensiveness than statements where the behaviour is compared to an accepted standard. For example, the statement 'I don't like the way you dress', is an expression of a personal opinion and will probably create resistance, especially if the listener does not feel that the communicator's opinions are any more legitimate than his or her own. On the other hand, 'Your dress is not in keeping with the company dress code', or 'Everyone is expected to wear a tie to work', are comparisons with external standards that have some legitimacy. Feelings of defensiveness are less likely to arise since the problem, not the person, is being addressed. In addition, other people are more likely to support a statement based on a common standard.

On the other hand, effective supportive communicators need not avoid expressing personal opinions or feelings about the *behaviour* or *attitudes* of others, provided they are 'owned' – 'I feel unhappy about the way...' However, we need to keep in mind some further points, as listed below.

2. Establish common ground – supportive communication begins by establishing a starting point accepted and valued by both parties.

Rogers (1961), Dyer (1972) and others argue that the best interpersonal communications, and the best relationships, are based on congruence, that is, matching the communication, verbally and non-verbally, exactly to what the individual is thinking and feeling. A very elementary aspect of congruence is 'choosing the right time and place' for a communication and abandoning the communication if the time and place become unsuitable.

> We were told of a case where an employee had just received a very worrying report from his doctor and was attempting to tell his manager that he had to take time off for an operation. The manager, who was under time pressures himself, heard but did not listen to the employee's concerns and continued with what was a very minor disciplinary matter.

Two kinds of **incongruence** are possible. One is a mismatch between what one is experiencing and what one is aware of. For example, an individual may not even be aware that he or she is experiencing anger toward another person, even though the anger is really present. Therapists must frequently help individuals reach such congruence between experience and awareness. A second kind of incongruence, and the one more closely related to supportive communication, is a mismatch between what one feels and what one communicates. For example, an individual may be aware of a feeling of anger but deny having that feeling.

When coaching and counselling subordinates, genuine, honest statements are always better than artificial or dishonest statements. Managers who hold back their true feelings or opinions, or who don't express what is really on their minds, create the impression that a hidden agenda exists. Subordinates sense that there is something else which has not been said. Therefore, they trust the communicator less and focus on trying to work out what the hidden message is, not on listening or trying to improve. False impressions and miscommunication result. Rogers (1961) suggests that congruence in communication lies at the heart of a general law of interpersonal relationships.

> The greater the congruence of experience, awareness and communication on the part of one individual, the more the ensuing relationship will involve: a tendency toward reciprocal communication with increasing congruence; a tendency toward more mutually accurate understanding of the communication; improved psychological adjustment and functioning in both parties; mutual satisfaction in the relationship.
>
> Conversely, the greater the communicated incongruence of experience and awareness, the more the ensuing relationship will involve further communication of the same quality; disintegration of accurate understanding; less adequate psychological adjustment and functioning in both parties; mutual dissatisfaction in the relationship.

Striving for congruence, of course, does not mean that one should let off steam immediately on getting upset, nor does it mean that one cannot repress certain inappropriate feelings (e.g., anger, disappointment, aggression). Other principles of supportive communication must also be practised, and achieving congruence at the expense of all other considerations is not productive. On the other hand, in problematic interactions, when reactive feedback must be given, individuals are more likely to express too little congruence than too much. This is because many people are afraid to respond in a completely honest way, or are not sure how to communicate congruently without being offensive. Saying exactly what one feels can sometimes offend the other person.

Consider the problem of a subordinate who is not performing up to expectation and displays a nonchalant attitude when given hints that the whole team is being affected. What could the superior say that would strengthen the relationship with the subordinate and still resolve the problem? How can one express honest feelings and opinions and still remain problem-focused, not person-focused? How can one be completely honest without offending another person? Other principles of supportive communication provide some guidelines.

3. 'Judge not or you will be judged' – supportive communication is descriptive, not evaluative.

When individuals use evaluative communication they make a judgement or place a label on other individuals or on their behaviour – 'You are bad', 'You are doing it wrong', 'You are incompetent'. This evaluation generally makes the other person feel under attack and respond defensively. Probable responses are, 'No, I'm not bad', 'I'm not doing it wrong', 'I am as competent as you are', 'You made me do it'. Arguments, bad feelings, exchanging blame and a weakening of the interpersonal relationship result.

The tendency to evaluate others is strongest when the issue is charged with emotion or when a person feels personally threatened. When people have strong feelings about an issue or experience anxiety as a result of a situation, they have a tendency to make negative evaluations of others' behaviour. Sometimes they try to resolve their own feelings or reduce their own anxiety by placing a label on others – 'You are bad, and that implies I am good. Therefore, I feel better'. At other times they may have such strong feelings that they want to punish the other person for violating their expectations or standards.

The problem with this approach is that evaluative communication is likely to be self-perpetuating. Placing a label on another individual generally leads that person to respond by placing a label on you, which makes you defensive in return. The accuracy of the communication as well as the strength of the relationship deteriorates.

An alternative to evaluation is the use of **descriptive communication**. Because is it difficult to avoid evaluating other people without some alternative strategy, the use of descriptive communication helps eliminate the tendency to evaluate or to perpetuate a defensive interaction. Descriptive communication involves three steps, summarised in Table 3.

Table 3   Descriptive communication

STEP 1:
- Describe as objectively as possible the event, behaviour or circumstance.
- Avoid accusations.
- Present data or evidence, if needed.

STEP 2:
- Describe your own reactions to or feelings about the event, behaviour or circumstance.
- Describe the objective consequences that have or will likely result.
- Focus on the behaviour and on your own reaction, not on the other individual or his or her personal attributes.

STEP 3:
- Suggest a more acceptable alternative.

First, describe as objectively as possible the event that occurred or the behaviour that needs to be modified. This description should be objective in that it relies on elements of the behaviour that could be confirmed by another person. Behaviour, as mentioned before, should be compared to accepted standards rather than to personal opinions or preferences. Subjective impressions or attributions to the motives of another person are not helpful in describing the event. The description 'You have finished fewer projects this month than anyone else in the division' can be confirmed (an objective record can be made available) and relates strictly to the behaviour and to an objective standard, not to the motives or personal characteristics of the subordinate. There is less likelihood of the subordinate feeling threatened, since no evaluative label is placed on the behaviour and no attack is being made on the person. Describing a behaviour, as opposed to evaluating a behaviour, is relatively neutral.

Second, describe reactions to the behaviour or its consequences. Rather than projecting onto another person the cause of the problem, the focus should be on the reactions or consequences the behaviour has produced. This requires that communicators be aware of their own reactions and be able to describe them. Using one-word descriptions for feelings is often the best method, for example, 'I'm concerned about our productivity'. Similarly, the consequences of the behaviour can be pointed out – 'Profits are low this month', 'Department quality ratings are down'. Describing feelings or consequences also lessens the likelihood of defensiveness since the problem is framed in the context of the communicator's feelings or objective consequences, not in the attributes of the subordinate. If those feelings or consequences are not described in an accusing way, the major energies of the communicators can be focused on problem-solving rather than on defending against evaluations.

Third, suggest a more acceptable alternative. This helps the other person save face (Goffman, 1955) and feel valued (Sieburg, 1978) by separating the individual from the behaviour. The self-esteem of the person is preserved; it is just the behaviour that should be modified. Care should be taken not to give the message 'I don't like the way things are, so what are you going to do about it?' The change need not be the responsibility of only one of the communicating parties. Rather, the emphasis should be on finding a solution that is acceptable to both, not on deciding who is right and who is wrong, or who should change and who shouldn't, for example, 'I'd like to suggest that we meet regularly to help you complete six more projects than last month'.

Blanchard and Johnson (1983) in their series of influential management monographs suggest certain very firm guidelines for giving negative criticism:

- Warn the person involved before the meeting and have the meeting as soon as possible
- Be specific about your criticism – detail the behaviour

- Express your feelings in no uncertain terms – anger, sorrow, shame, disappointment
- Allow your feelings to register with the other person
- Outline what they have to do
- Re-establish the relationship – it is the behaviour that is wrong not the person concerned
- Close the meeting and the subject once and for all. The whole interview should take less than one minute.

One concern that is sometimes expressed regarding descriptive communication is that these steps may not work unless the other person shares your values and knows the rules. For example, the other person might say, 'I don't care how you feel,' or 'I have an excuse for what happened, so it's not my fault.'

If the manager and the subordinate cannot work on the problem together, no amount of communication about the consequences of poor performance will be productive. Instead, the focus of the communication should be shifted to the obstacles that inhibit working together to improve performance.

Effective managers never abandon the three steps. They simply switch the focus. They might respond: 'I'm surprised to hear you say that you don't care how I feel about this problem' (Step 1); 'Your response worries me, I think it might have important implications for the work of our team' (Step 2); and 'I suggest we spend some time trying to identify the obstacles you feel might be inhibiting our ability to work together on this problem' (Step 3).

It has been our experience that few individuals are negative about justifiable criticism, if correctly presented – method, time and place. Most people are professionals who wish to do and be seen to do a good job. These are core Theory Y assumptions (McGregor, 1960) as opposed to Theory X assumptions, such as 'employees are to be mistrusted' and 'it takes a sharp stick to motivate change'. In our experience, most people want to do better, to perform successfully and to be contributors. When managers use supportive communication principles not as manipulative devices but as genuine techniques to foster development and improvement, we have seldom found that people will not accept these genuine, congruent expressions.

It is important to keep in mind, however, that the steps of descriptive communication do not imply that one person should do all the changing. Frequently, a middle ground must be reached on which both individuals are satisfied (e.g., one person becomes more tolerant of slow work, and the other person becomes more conscious of trying to work faster). Also, when it is necessary to make evaluative statements, the evaluations should be made in terms of some established criteria (e.g., 'Your behaviour does not meet the prescribed standard'), probable outcomes (e.g., 'Continuation of your behaviour will lead to worse consequences'), or less appropriate behaviour by the same person (e.g., 'This behaviour is not as good as your past behaviour'). The important point is to avoid patronising the other person or arousing defensiveness.

4. Supportive communication validates rather than invalidates individuals – don't put people down.

Even though it is descriptive, communication may still be destructive. Barnlund (1968) observed:

> People do not take time, do not listen, do not try to understand, but interrupt, anticipate, criticise or disregard what is said; in their own remarks they are frequently vague, inconsistent, verbose, insincere or dogmatic. As a result, people often conclude conversations feeling more inadequate, more misunderstood and more alienated than when they started.

The key in our experience is to treat people as adults, unless you have very strong evidence that this is not so, and to act naturally.

> A personnel manager of a large company was well known as a 'dour' Scot – he never joked and was know as 'an ill wind that brings nobody any good'. He was however efficient and respected. He was sent on a course on supportive communication and returned with the objective of empowering the staff.
>
> One of his first gross failures was with a senior and highly effective, personal assistant to a colleague. He started the phone conversation by asking whether she wanted the good news or the bad news first. The bemused lady, who did not know about the training course, asked for the bad news and was told that she had sent a memo out with a typographical error. He then went on to the good news which was that she

had been regraded and would receive a substantial pay increase. She only heard the bad news and was in tears to her manager because she thought she had been sacked.

Communication that is invalidating arouses negative feelings about self-worth, identity and relatedness to others. It denies the presence, uniqueness or importance of other individuals. Especially important are communications that invalidate people by conveying superiority, rigidity and indifference (Sieburg, 1978; Galbraith, 1975; Gibb, 1961). Communication that is based on assumptions of grade or seniority gives the impression that the communicator is informed while others are ignorant, adequate while others are inadequate, competent while others are incompetent, or powerful while others are impotent. It creates a barrier between the communicator and those to whom the message is sent.

Communication based on a feeling of superiority can take the form of put-downs, in which others are made to look bad so that the communicator looks good. Or it can take the form of 'one-upmanship', in which the communicator tries to elevate himself or herself in the esteem of others.

- One common form of downward communication based on status is the use of **jargon**, acronyms, or words used in such a way as to exclude others or create barriers in a relationship. Doctors, lawyers, government employees and many other professionals are well known for their use of jargon or acronyms to exclude others, or to elevate themselves rather than to clarify a message. Speaking a foreign language in the presence of people who don't understand it also creates the impression of superiority. In most circumstances, using words or language that a listener can't understand is simply bad manners.

- **Rigidity** in communication is the second major type of invalidation: The communication is portrayed as absolute, unequivocal or unquestionable. No other opinion or point of view could possibly be considered. Individuals who communicate in dogmatic, 'know-it-all' ways often do so in order to minimise others' contributions or to invalidate others' perspectives. It is possible to communicate rigidity, however, in ways other than just being dogmatic. Rigidity is communicated, for example, by:

1. Never expressing agreement with anyone else, or when agreement is expressed, expressing it in terms of they 'agree with me', not 'I agree with them'.
2. Reinterpreting all other viewpoints to conform to one's own.
3. Never saying, 'I don't know', but having an answer for everything.
4. Not expressing openness to others' opinions or information.
5. Using evaluative and invalidating statements, instead of communicating understanding and validation for others.
6. Appearing unwilling to tolerate criticism or alternative points of view.
7. Reducing complex issues to simplistic definitions.
8. Using all-encompassing and over-generalised statements (that is, communicating the message that everything worthwhile that can be said about the subject has just been said).
9. Merging definitions of problems with solutions so alternatives are not considered.
10. Placing exclamation points after statements creating the impression that the statement is final, complete or unqualified.

■ **Indifference** is communicated when the other person's existence or importance is not acknowledged. A person may do this by using silence, by making no verbal response to the other's statements, by avoiding eye contact or any facial expression, by interrupting the other person frequently, by using impersonal words ('one should not' instead of 'you should not'), or by engaging in unrelated activity during a conversation. The communicator appears not to care about the other person and gives the impression of being impervious to the other person's feelings or perspective.

■ **Imperviousness** (Sieburg, 1978) means that the communicator does not acknowledge the feelings or opinions of the other person. They are either labelled illegitimate, for example, 'You shouldn't feel that way', or they are labelled as naive, for example, 'You don't understand', or (worse still) 'Your opinion is uninformed'.

34 *Developing Management Skills*

Communication is invalidating when it denies the other person an opportunity to establish a mutually satisfying relationship – when contributions cannot be made by both parties. When one person doesn't allow the other to finish a sentence, adopts a competitive, win-or-lose stance, sends confusing messages or disqualifies the other person from making a contribution, communication is invalidating and, therefore, dysfunctional for effective problem-solving.

■ **Invalidating communication**, then, 'reflects unawareness of others, misconception of them, rejection of their attempt to communicate, denial of their self-experience, or disaffiliation with them' (Sieburg, 1978). Invalidation is even more destructive in coaching and counselling than criticism or disagreement, because criticism and disagreement validate the other person by recognising that what was said or done is worthy of correction, response or at least notice (Jacobs, 1973). As William James (1965) stated, 'No more fiendish punishment could be devised, even were such a thing physically possible, than that one could be turned loose in a society and remain absolutely unnoticed by all the members thereof.'

We abandoned an exercise to demonstrate this point when it proved too effective. In the exercise, five volunteers are assembled from a group of managers in a training course. The first in the group is praised for being him or herself – 'It's great to have a really positive person in a group – now sit down.' The second is praised for completing a trivial act well – clapping in tune. The third is given a further trivial task – clapping the rhythm of a nursery rhyme – and is admonished for not being very good at the task. The fourth person is dismissed personally – 'Why you volunteered is beyond me, you are the sort of person who learns nothing from management courses.'

When the four are seated, at various levels of discontent, the tutor resumed the session, leaving the fifth standing. After a few minutes a range of things may have happened. The ignored fifth person may have become hostile, crept back to his or her seat, or simply stayed looking awkward.

We then debrief the five people. The one who was really hurt was not the one who was told off – the one who was ignored feels the worst. On one occasion, the man felt so bad about being left and ignored that we abandoned using the demonstration on all subsequent courses. He was HURT.

■ **Validating communication**, on the other hand, helps people feel recognised, understood, accepted and valued. It has three attributes:
1. It is egalitarian
2. It is flexible
3. It is two-way based on agreement

Egalitarian communication (the opposite of status-based communication) is especially important when a manager coaches or counsels a subordinate. When a hierarchical distinction exists between coaches/counsellors and subordinates, it is easy for subordinates to feel invalidated since they have access to less power and information than their manager. Supportive communicators, however, help subordinates feel that they have a stake in identifying problems and resolving them, by communicating an egalitarian stance. They treat subordinates as worthwhile, competent and insightful, and emphasise joint problem-solving rather than project a superior position. One way they do this is by using flexible (rather than rigid) statements.

Flexibility in communication is the willingness of the coach or counsellor to accept that additional data and other alternatives may exist, or that other individuals may be able to make significant contributions both to solving the problem and to the relationship. Flexible communication is communicating with genuine humility and openness to new insight. As Bertrand Russell stated, 'One's certainty varies inversely with one's knowledge.' Disraeli noted that 'To be conscious that you are ignorant is a first great step toward knowledge.' We might say that only an expert is aware that there is more to learn.

Perceptions and opinions are not presented as facts in flexible communication, but are stated provisionally. That is, a distinction is made between facts and opinions, between evidence and assumptions, and no claim is made for the truthfulness of opinions. Rather, they are identified as being changeable if more data should become available. Flexible communication conveys a

willingness to enter into joint problem-solving rather than to
control the other person or to assume a master-teacher role. Being
flexible is not synonymous with being wishy-washy.

A witness being sworn in at a trial, as reported by Haney
(1979), exemplified the ultimate flexibility:

> **Court Clerk:** Do you swear to tell the truth, the whole truth, and
> nothing but the truth, so help you God?
> **Witness:** Look, if I knew the truth, the whole truth, and nothing but
> the truth, I would be God!

Two-way communication is an implied result of egalitarianism and
flexibility. Individuals feel validated when they are asked questions, given time to express their opinions, and encouraged to par-
ticipate actively in the coaching and counselling session. Two-way
interchange simply communicates the message that subordinates
are valued by the manager and that the process of coaching and
counselling is best accomplished in an atmosphere of teamwork.
We discuss the issue at length in the book from the series – *Effective Motivation.*

5. Be specific and not global.

In general, the more specific a statement is, the more useful it is. For
example, the statement, 'You're a poor time manager' is too general
to be useful, whereas 'You spent an hour scheduling meetings today
when that could have been done by your assistant' provides specific
information that can serve as a basis for behavioural change.

Specific statements avoid extremes and absolutes. The following are extreme statements that lead to defensiveness or a feeling
of being put-down:

> A: 'You never ask for my advice.'
> B: 'Yes I do; I always consult you before making a decision.'
> A: 'You have no consideration for others' feelings.'
> B: 'I do. I am very considerate.'
> A: 'This job stinks.'
> B: 'You're wrong. It's a great job.'

Another common type of general communication is the either-or
statement, such as, 'You either do what I say or I'll fire you'.

The uselessness of polarised statements lies in their denial of any alternatives. The possible responses of the recipient of the communication are severely constrained. About the only response to such a statement is to contradict or deny it, and this simply leads to defensiveness and arguments. A statement in 1931 by Adolf Hitler illustrates the point: 'Everyone in Germany is a National Socialist – the few outside the party are either lunatics or idiots'. Specific statements are more useful in coaching and counselling because they focus on behavioural events and indicate gradations in positions. More useful forms of the examples above are the following:

A: 'You made that decision yesterday without asking for my advice.'

B: 'Yes, I did. While I generally like to get your opinion, I didn't think it was necessary in this case.'

A: 'By using sarcasm in your response to my request, you gave me the impression that you don't care about my feelings.'

B: 'I'm sorry, I know I am often sarcastic without thinking how it affects others.'

A: 'It's difficult to hear in this lecture room.'

B: 'That may be so, but I find the instructor's illustrations very helpful.'

As these examples point out, the use of qualifier words such as 'generally', 'frequently', 'appears to be', ' may be', etc., help avoid general connotations, as does linking the statement to a specific event. To illustrate this point, list antonyms for each of the following words.

good _____   happy _____

light _____   hot _____

You probably found this relatively simple. Now take the same words and provide some gradations between the two extremes. The middle words will be more specific than the two words on the ends of the continuum.

good	_____	_____	_____	_____	bad
happy	_____	_____	_____	_____	sad
light	_____	_____	_____	_____	dark
hot	_____	_____	_____	_____	cold

Not all specific statements are useful just because they are grounded in a personal experience of need to be qualified in some way. Specific statements may not be useful if they focus on things over which another person has no control. 'I hate it when it rains', for example, may relieve some personal frustration, but the referent of the statement is something about which little can be done. The communication is not very useful. Similarly, communicating the message (even implicitly) 'I don't like people of your background' or 'Your personality bothers me' only prove frustrating for the interacting individuals. Such statements are usually interpreted as personal attacks. Specific communication is useful to the extent that it focuses on an identifiable problem or behaviour about which something can be done (e.g., 'It bothers me that you checked up on me four times today').

6. There is a time and a place for everything – supportive communication needs to be part of the general flow and not something that stands out.

Supportive communication should be conjunctive and not disjunctive. Communication can appear disjunctive in at least three ways.

■ First, there can be a lack of equal opportunity to speak. When one person interrupts another, when someone dominates by controlling 'air time', or when two or more people try to speak at the same time, the communication is disjunctive. The transitions between speeches simply do not flow smoothly.

■ Second, extended pauses are disjunctive. When speakers pause for long periods in the middle of their speeches or when there are long pauses before responses, the communication is disjunctive. Pauses need not be total silence; the space may be filled with 'umm', 'aaah', or a repetition of something stated earlier.

- Third, topic control can be disjointed. When one person decides unilaterally what the topic of conversation will be (as opposed to having it decided bilateral), the communication is disjunctive. Individuals may switch topics, for example, with no reference to what was just said, or they may control the other person's communication topic by directing what should be responded to. Sieburg (1969) found that more than 25 per cent of the statements made in small-group discussions failed to refer to or even acknowledge previous speakers or their statements.

These three factors – taking turns at speaking, management of timing and topic control – contribute to what has been called 'interaction management'. They have been found to be critical to effective supportive communication. In an empirical study of per-ceived communication competence, it has been found that the smoother the management of the interaction [of the three factors above], the more competent the communicator was perceived to be. In fact, interaction management was concluded to be the most powerful determinant of perceived communication competence in his experimental study. Individuals who used conjunctive commu-nication were rated as being significantly more competent in inter-personal communication than were those whose communication was disjunctive. By using conjunctive communication, they con-firm the worth of the other person's statements, thereby helping to foster joint problem-solving and teamwork.

Skilled coaches and counsellors use several kinds of behaviours in managing communication situations so they are conjunctive rather than disjunctive. For example, they foster conjunctive com-munication in an interaction by asking questions that are based directly on the subordinate's previous statement, by waiting for a sentence to be completed before beginning a response (for ex-ample, not finishing a sentence for someone else), and by saying only two or three sentences at a time before pausing to give the other person a chance to add input. In addition, they avoid long pauses, their statements refer to what has been said before and they take turns at speaking. Figure 3 illustrates that a continuum may exist for conjunctive statements.

For example, statements that relate to the immediately preceding statement are most conjunctive; statements that relate to something that occurred earlier in the conversation are somewhat less so; statements that relate to something that both parties share in common are less conjunctive still; and statements that relate to none of these factors are the least conjunctive.

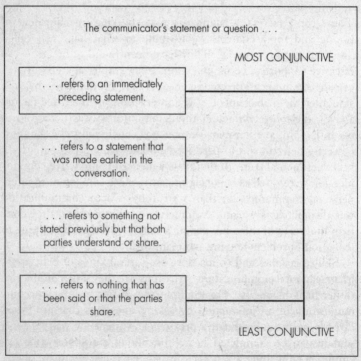

FIGURE 3 A continuum of conjunctive statements

7. Remember YOU are paid to do the job – never delegate upward and even imply personal disloyalty.

Supportive communication is owned, not disowned. Taking responsibility for one's statements, acknowledging that the source of the ideas is oneself and not another person or group is owning communication. Using first-person words, such as 'I', 'me', 'mine', indicates owning communication. Disowning communication is suggested by use of third-person or first-person-plural words – 'We think', 'They said', or 'One might say'. Disowned communication is attributed to an unknown person, group, or to some external source (e.g., 'Lots of people think'). The communicator avoids taking responsibility for the message and therefore avoids investing in the interaction. This conveys the message that the communicator is aloof or uncaring about the receiver, or is not confident enough in the ideas expressed to take responsibility for them.

Glasser (1965) based his approach to therapy on the concept of responsibility for, or owning, communication and behaviour. According to Glasser, individuals are mentally healthy if they accept responsibility for their statements and behaviours. They are ill if they avoid taking responsibility. According to this theory, taking responsibility for one's communication builds self-confidence and a sense of self-worth in the communicator. It also builds confidence in the receiver of the communication by confirming that his or her worth is valued.

One result of disowning communication is that the listener is never sure whose point of view the message represents and is apt to misinterpret it – 'How can I respond if I don't know to whom I am responding to?' Moreover, an implicit message associated with disowned communication is, 'I want to keep distance between you and me'. The speaker communicates as a representative rather than as a person, or as a message-conveyer rather than as an interested individual. Owning communication, on the other hand, indicates a willingness to invest oneself in the relationship and to act as a colleague or helper.

8. Supportive communication is not a one-way street –

always be prepared to listen and act on what you hear; never be dismissive.

The previous seven attributes of supportive communication all focus on message delivery, where a message is initiated by the coach or counsellor. But another aspect of supportive communication which is at least as important as delivering supportive messages, is listening and responding effectively to someone else's statements. As Maier, Solem and Maier (1973) stated, 'In any conversation, the person who talks the most is the one who learns the least about the other person. The good supervisor therefore must become a good listener.'

In a survey of personnel directors in 300 businesses and industries, conducted to determine what skills are most important in becoming a manager, Crocker (1978) reported that effective listening was ranked highest. Despite its importance in managerial success, however, and despite the fact that most people spend at least 45 per cent of their communication time listening, most people have under-developed listening skills. Tests have shown, for example, that individuals are usually about 25 per cent effective in listening (Huseman, Lahiff and Hatfield, 1976), that is, they listen to and understand only about a quarter, on average, of what is being communicated. Even when asked to rate the extent to which they are skilled listeners, 85 per cent of all individuals rate themselves as average or worse. Only 5 per cent rate themselves as highly skilled (Steil, 1980). It is particularly unfortunate that listening skills are poorest when people interact with those closest to them, such as family members and colleagues.

When individuals are preoccupied with meeting their own needs (e.g., saving face, persuading someone else, winning a point, avoiding getting involved), when they have already made a judgement, or when they hold negative attitudes toward the communicator or the message, they can't listen effectively. Because a person listens at the rate of 500 words a minute but speaks at a normal rate of only 125 to 250 words a minute, the listener's mind can dwell on other things half the time. Therefore, being a good listener is neither easy nor automatic. It requires developing the ability to hear and understand the message sent by another person, while at the same time helping to strengthen the relationship between the interacting parties.

Rogers and Farson (1976) suggest that this kind of listening conveys the idea that 'I'm interested in you as a person, and I think what you feel is important. I respect your thoughts, and even if I don't agree with them, I know they are valid for you. I feel sure you have a contribution to make. I think you're worth listening to, and I want you to know that I'm the kind of person you can talk to'.

People do not know they are being listened to unless the listener makes some type of response. Competent managers who must coach and counsel, select carefully from a repertoire of response alternatives that clarify the communication as well as strengthen the interpersonal relationship. The mark of a supportive listener is the competence to select appropriate responses to others' statements.

The appropriateness of a response depends largely on whether the focus of the interaction is primarily coaching or counselling. Of course, seldom can these two activities be separated from one another completely. Effective coaching often involves counselling, and effective counselling sometimes involves coaching. Attentive listening, however, involves the use of a variety of responses, some being more appropriate under certain circumstances than others.

Figure 4 (next page) lists four major response types and arranges them on a continuum from most directive and closed to the most non-directive or open. Closed responses eliminate discussion of topics and provide direction to individuals. They represent methods by which the listener can control the topic of conversation. Open responses, on the other hand, allow the communicator, not the listener, to control the topic of conversation. Each of these response types has certain advantages and disadvantages, and none are appropriate all the time under all circumstances.

Most people get into the habit of relying heavily on one or two response types, and they use them regardless of the circumstances. Moreover, most people have been found to rely first and foremost on evaluative or judgmental responses (Rogers, 1961). That is, when they encounter another person's statements, most people tend to agree or disagree, pass judgement, or immediately form a

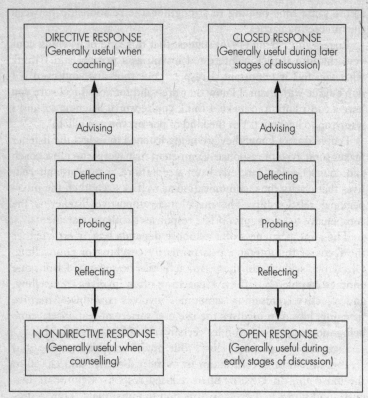

FIGURE 4   Responsive types in supportive listening

personal opinion about the legitimacy or veracity of the statement. On average, only about 80 per cent of most people's responses have been found to be evaluative. Supportive listening, however, avoids evaluation and judgement as a first response. Instead, it relies on flexibility in response types and the appropriate match of responses to circumstances. Here are the four response types indicating active listening:

- Advising
- Deflecting
- Probing
- Reflecting

Advising

An advising response is a response that provides direction, evaluation, personal opinion or instruction. Such a response imposes on the communicator the point of view of the listener, and it creates listener control over the topic of conversation. The advantages of an advising response are that it helps the communicator understand something that may have been unclear before, it helps identify a solution to a problem, and it can provide clarity about how the communicator should feel or act in the future. It is most appropriate when the listener has expertise that the communicator doesn't possess or when the communicator is in need of direction. Supportive listening sometimes means that the listener does the talking, but this is usually appropriate only when advice or direction is specifically requested. Most listeners have a tendency to offer much more advice and direction than is appropriate.

One problem with advising is that it can produce dependence. Individuals get used to having someone else generate the answers, directions or clarification. They are not permitted to work out the issues and the solutions for themselves. A second problem is that advising also creates the impression that the communicator is not being understood by the listener. Rogers (1961) found that most people, even when they seem to be asking for advice, mainly desire understanding and acceptance, not advice. They want the listener to share in the communication, but not take charge of it. The problem with advising is that it removes from the communicator control of the conversation; it focuses attention on the advice itself rather than on the communicator's problem. A third problem with advising is that it shifts focus from the communicator's message to the listener's advice. When listeners feel advising is appropriate, they concentrate more on the legitimacy of the advice or on the generation of alternatives and solutions than on simply listening attentively. When listeners are expected to generate advice and direction, they may focus more on their own experience than on the communicator's. A fourth potential problem with advising is that it can imply that communicators don't have sufficient understanding, expertise, insight or maturity – i.e., that they are in need of help because of incompetence.

One way to help overcome these disadvantages of advising is to not use advising as a first response in coaching and counselling.

> One concept we find is useful is that of seeing yourself as working with your ears – listening and not participating except to encourage and collate; working with your hands – showing others how to do things by example; and working with your mouth – advising. All need to be used appropriately. Sticking to one channel – ears, hands or mouth – all the time can be very ineffectual.

Responses that allow communicators to have control over the topics of conversation, that show understanding and acceptance, and that encourage self-reliance on the part of communicators have their place. In addition, the advice that is given should either be connected to an accepted standard (e.g., you are expected to) or it should be equivocal. An accepted standard means that communicators and listeners both acknowledge that the advice will lead to a desired outcome and that it is inherently good, right or appropriate. When this is impossible, the advice should be communicated as the listener's opinion or feeling, and as only one option (i.e., with flexibility), not as the only option. This permits communicators to accept or reject the advice without feeling that the advisor is being invalidated or rejected if the advice is not accepted.

Deflecting

A deflecting response switches the focus from the communicator's problem to one selected by the listener. It simply means that the listener changes the subject. Listeners may substitute their own experience for that of the communicator (e.g., 'Let me tell you something similar that happened to me.') or introduce an entirely new topic (e.g., 'That reminds me of [something else].'). The listener may think the current problem is unclear to the communicator and the use of examples or analogies will help. Or the listener may feel that the communicator needs to be reassured that others have experienced the same problem and that support and understanding are available.

Deflecting responses are most appropriate when a comparison or reassurance is needed. They can provide empathy and support by communicating the message, 'I understand because of what happened to me (or someone else)'. They can also convey assurance that, 'Things will be fine. Others have also had this experience'. Deflection is also often used to avoid embarrassing either the communicator or the listener. Changing the subject when either party gets uncomfortable and answering a question other than the one asked are common examples.

The disadvantages of deflecting responses, however, are that they can imply that the communicator's message is not important or that the experience of the listener is more significant than that of the communicator. It may produce competitiveness or feelings of being 'one-upped' by the listener. Deflection can be interpreted as, 'My experience is more worthy of discussion than yours'. Or it may simply change the subject from something that is important and central to the communicator, to a topic that is not important.

Deflecting responses are most effective when they are conjunctive – when they are clearly connected to what the communicator just said, when the listener's response leads directly back to the communicator's concerns, and when the reason for the deflection is made clear. That is, deflecting can produce desirable outcomes in coaching and counselling if the communicator feels supported and understood, not invalidated, by the change in topic focus.

Probing
A probing response asks a question about what the communicator just said or about a topic selected by the listener. The intent of a probe is to acquire additional information, to help the communicator say more about the topic, or to help the listener foster more appropriate responses. For example, an effective way to avoid being evaluative and judgmental, and to avoid triggering defensive reactions is to continue to ask questions. Questioning helps the listener adopt the communicator's frame of reference so that in coaching situations suggestions can be specific (not general) and in counselling situations statements can be descriptive (not evaluative). Questions tend to be more neutral in tone than direct statements.

Questioning, however, can sometimes have the unwelcome effect of switching the focus of attention from the communicator's statement to the reasons behind it. The question 'Why do you think that?', for example, might force the communicator to justify

a feeling or a perception rather than just report it. Similarly, probing responses can serve as a mechanism for escaping discussion of
a topic or for manoeuvring the topic around to one the listener
wants to discuss (e.g., 'Instead of discussing your feelings about
your job, tell me why you didn't respond to my memo'). Probing
responses can also allow the communicator to lose control of the
conversation, especially when difficult subjects need to be
addressed (e.g., 'I'll only talk about those things about which you
ask me about').

Two important points should be kept in mind to make probing
more effective. One is that 'why' questions are seldom as effective
as 'what' questions. 'Why' questions lead to topic changes, escape
and speculation more often than to valid information. For example, the question, 'Why do you feel that way?' can lead to statements such as 'Because my id is not sufficiently controlled by my
ego' or 'Because my father was an alcoholic and my mother beat
me'. These are extreme examples, but they illustrate how ineffective 'why' questions can be. 'What do you mean by that?' is likely
to be more fruitful.

A second hint is to tailor the probes to fit the situation. When
the communicator's statement does not contain enough information or part of the message is not understood, an elaboration probe
should be used (e.g., 'Can you tell me more about that?'). When
the message is not clear or is ambiguous, a clarification probe is
best (e.g., 'What do you mean by that?'). A repetition probe
should be used when the communicator is avoiding a topic or
hasn't answered a previous question (e.g., 'Once again, what do
you think about that'). A reflective probe is most effective when
the communicator is being encouraged to keep pursuing the same
topic in greater depth (e.g., 'You say you are discouraged?'). Probing responses are especially effective in turning potentially hostile
situations into productive conversations. Asking questions can
often turn attacks into consensus, evaluations into descriptions,
general statements into specific statements, or person-focused
declarations into problem-focused declarations. In other words,
probes can often be used to help others use supportive communication when they have not been trained in advance to do so.

Reflecting

The primary purpose of the reflecting response is to mirror back to the communicator the message that was heard, and to communicate understanding and acceptance of the person. Reflecting the message in different words allows the speaker to feel listened to, understood and free to explore the topic in more depth. Reflective responding involves paraphrasing and clarifying the message. Instead of simply mimicking the communication, supportive listeners contribute meaning, understanding and acceptance to the conversation while still allowing communicators to pursue topics of their choosing. Rogers (1961), Benjamin (1969), Athos and Gabarro (1978) and others argue that this response should be used most of the time in coaching and counselling since it leads to the most clear communication and the most supportive relationships.

A potential disadvantage of reflective responses is that communicators can get the opposite impression to the one intended. That is, they can get the feeling that they are not being understood or listened to carefully. If they keep hearing reflections of what they just said, their response might begin to be, 'I just said that. Aren't you listening to me?' Reflective responses, in other words, can be perceived as 'a technique' or as a superficial response to a message.

The most effective listeners keep the following rules in mind when using reflective responses.

1. Avoid repeating the same response over and over, such as 'You feel that . . . ?', 'Are you saying that . . . ?' or 'What I heard you say was . . .'.
2. Avoid an exchange in which listeners do not contribute equally to the conversation, but serve only as mimics. (One can use understanding/reflective responses while still taking equal responsibility for the depth and meaning of the communication.)
3. Respond to the personal rather than the impersonal. For example, to a complaint by a subordinate about close supervision and feelings of incompetence and annoyance, an understanding/reflective response would focus on personal feelings rather than on supervision style.
4. Respond to expressed feelings before responding to content. When expressed, feelings are the most important part of the

message to the person, and may stand in the way of the ability to communicate clearly.

5. Respond with empathy and acceptance. Avoid the extremes of complete objectivity, detachment or distance on the one hand, or over-identification (accepting the feelings as one's own) on the other.

6. Avoid expressing agreement or disagreement with the statements.

The Personal Management Interview

The preceding eight attributes of supportive communication are effective for our 'normal' life as well as the professional interactions between managers and their subordinates. One important difference between effective and ineffective managers is the extent to which they provide their subordinates with opportunities to receive regular feedback, to feel supported and bolstered, and to be coached and counselled. Providing these opportunities is difficult, however, because of the tremendous time demands most managers face. Many managers want to coach, counsel and train subordinates, but simply never find the time. Therefore, one important mechanism for applying supportive communication and for providing subordinates with development and feedback opportunities, is to implement a personal management interview programme. Most of the companies with which we deal have an annual appraisal programme. However, there are several problems in training managers to conduct appraisal interviews, as follows:

- Annual appraisal is not a substitute for good management. An annual appraisal should be a confirmation and collation of what has gone before. In some companies it is the *only* time in the year when the manager has to confront dysfunctional behaviour. Once a year is not enough.

- The annual appraisal is always, in our experience, tied into some organisational objectives – grading, salary review, succession planning. Since these formal objectives *have* to be met, the less formal issue of human relationships may get side-tracked.

A personal management interview programme is a regularly scheduled, one-to-one meeting between a manager and his or her subordinates without the organisational pressures of the annual appraisal. In a study of the performance of intact departments and teams in a variety of organisations, Boss (1983) found that effectiveness increased significantly when managers conducted regular, private meetings with subordinates on a bi-weekly or monthly basis. These meetings were referred to as 'personal management interviews'.

Instituting a personal management interview programme consists of two steps:

1. **First, a session is held in which expectations, responsibilities, standards of evaluation, reporting relationships, and so on, are clarified.** Unless such a meeting is held, most subordinates do not have a clear idea of exactly what is expected of them or on what basis they will be evaluated. In our own experiences with managers and executives, few have expressed confidence that they know precisely what is expected of them or how they are being evaluated in their jobs. In this first session, that uncertainty is overcome; the manager and subordinate negotiate all job-related issues that are not prescribed by policy or by mandate. A written record should be made of the agreements and responsibilities that result from the meetings and this can serve as an informal contract between the manager and the subordinate. The goal of a role-negotiation session is to obtain clarity between both parties regarding what each expects from the other. Because this role negotiation is not adversarial but rather focuses on supportiveness and team-building, the eight supportive communication principles should characterise the interaction.

2. **The second (and most important) step in a personal management interview plan is a programme of ongoing, one-to-one meetings of the manager with each subordinate.** These meetings are regular (not just when a mistake is made or a crisis arises) and private (not overheard by others). This meeting provides managers with the opportunity to coach and counsel subordinates and to help them improve their own

skills and job performance. Therefore, each meeting should last from 45–60 minutes and focus on items such as the following: (1) managerial and organisational problems, (2) information sharing, (3) interpersonal issues, (4) obstacles to improvement, (5) training in management skills, (6) individual needs, (7) feedback on job performance and (8) personal concerns or problems.

The meeting always leads toward action items to be accomplished before the next meeting, some by the subordinate and others by the manager. Both parties prepare for the meeting and both bring items to be discussed. It is not a formal appraisal session called by the manager, but a development and improvement session in which both the manager and subordinate have a stake. It is a chance for subordinates to have personal time with the manager to work out issues and report information; consequently, it helps eliminate unscheduled interruptions and long, inefficient group meetings. At each subsequent meeting, action items are reviewed from previous meetings, so that continuous improvement is always being encouraged. Table 4 summarises the characteristics of the personal management interview programme.

Boss's research found that a variety of benefits resulted in teams that instituted this programme. It not only increased their effectiveness, but improved individual accountability, department meeting efficiency and communication flows. Managers actually found more time available because it reduced interruptions and unscheduled meetings. Furthermore, participants defined it as a successful experience in itself. These results occurred, however, when principles of supportive communication characterised the manager's approach to the meetings. When correction or negative feedback had to be communicated, and when coaching or counselling was called for (which is typical of almost every manager–subordinate relationship at some point), supportive communication helped strengthen the interpersonal relationship at the same time that problems were solved and performance improved. In brief, setting aside time for formal, structured interaction between managers and their subordinates, in which supportive communication played a part, produced markedly improved performances.

Table 4   Characteristics of a personal management interview programme

1. The interview is regular and private.
2. The major intent of the meeting is continuous improvement in personal, interpersonal and organisational performance, so the meeting is action-oriented.
3. Both the manager and the subordinate prepare agenda items for the meeting. It is a meeting for both of them, not just for the manager.
4. Sufficient time is allowed for the interaction, usually about an hour.
5. Supportive communication is used so that joint problem-solving and continuous improvement result (in both task accomplishment and interpersonal relationships).
6. The first agenda item is a follow-up on the action items generated by the previous meeting.
7. Major agenda items for the meeting might include:
   - Managerial and organisational problems
   - Organisational values and vision
   - Information sharing
   - Interpersonal issues
   - Obstacles to improvement
   - Training in management skills
   - Individual needs
   - Feedback on job performance
   - Personal concerns and problems
8. Praise and encouragement are intermingled with problem-solving.
9. A review of action items generated by the meeting occurs at the end of the interview.

Summary

The most important barriers to effective communication in organisations are interpersonal. Much progress has been made in the last two decades in improving the accuracy of message delivery in organisations, but communication problems still persist between managers, their subordinates and peers (not to mention between most individuals in their daily interactions). A major reason for these problems is that the kind of communication used does not support a positive interpersonal relationship. Instead, it frequently engenders distrust, hostility, defensiveness, and feelings of incompetence and low self-esteem.

These results are seldom associated with situations in which compliments are given, congratulations are made, a bonus is awarded or other positive interactions occur. Most people have little trouble communicating effectively in such situations. Instead, potentially harmful communication patterns are most likely to emerge when one is giving feedback on poor performance, saying 'no' to a proposal or request, resolving a difference of opinion between two subordinates, correcting problem behaviours, receiving criticism from others, or facing other negative interactions. These situations also arise frequently in the context of coaching and counselling subordinates. Handling these situations in a way that fosters interpersonal growth and a strengthening of relationships is one mark of an effective manager.

In this book we have pointed out that effective communicators adhere to the principles of supportive communication, thus ensuring greater clarity and understanding of the message while making the other person feel accepted, valued and supported. Of course, it is possible to become overly concerned with technique in trying to incorporate these principles and thereby defeat the goal of being supportive. It is possible to become artificial, or incongruent, by focusing on technique rather than on honest, caring communication. But if the principles are practised and consciously implemented in everyday interactions, they can be important tools in helping improve your communication competence.

Behavioural Guidelines

The following behavioural guidelines will help you practise supportive communication:

1. Differentiate between coaching situations, where advice and direction are required, and counselling situations where the relative roles are much more equal, and understanding and consulting is needed.
2. Keep to the task or the problem – describe behaviours or events and not personalities.
3. Be honest – communicate using true feelings without acting them out in destructive ways.
4. Use descriptive, not evaluative statements: describe objectively what occurred; describe your reactions to the event and its objective consequences; and suggest an alternative that is acceptable to you.
5. Show that you value the other person and communicate that the relationship is important to you. Listen and be prepared to be flexible, revising your approach with what you hear. Encourage dialogue, identifying areas of agreement or positive characteristics

before working through areas of disagreement or negative factors.

6. Use specific statements rather than global (either–or, black–white) statements. Allow yourself the use of words that do not reflect absolutes; practice being flexible. Focus on the things that can be controlled – 'You are too tall' is hardly a criticism that others can act upon.
7. Use statements that flow smoothly from what was said previously; don't dominate the conversation; don't cause long pauses; and acknowledge what was said before.
8. Own your statements: use personal words ('I') rather than impersonal words ('they').
9. Demonstrate supportive listening: use a variety of responses to others' statements depending on whether you are coaching or counselling someone else, but with a bias toward reflecting responses.
10. Implement a personal management interview programme characterised by supportive communication, in order to coach, counsel and foster personal development among subordinates.

Skill Analysis

Cases Involving Coaching and Counselling

Find Somebody Else

Ron Davis, the relatively new general manager of the machine tooling group at Parker Manufacturing, was visiting one of the factories. He arranged a meeting with Mike Leonard, a plant manager who reported to him.

Ron: Mike, I've arranged this meeting with you because I've been reviewing performance data and I wanted to give you some feedback. I know we haven't talked face-to-face before, but I think it's time we review how you're doing. I'm afraid that some of things I have to say are not very favourable.

Mike: Well, since you're the new boss, I'll just have to listen. I've had meetings like this before with new people who come onto my site and think they know what's going on.

Ron: Look, Mike, I want this to be a two-way interchange. I'm not here to read an edict to you, and I'm not here to tell you how to do your job. There are just some areas for improvement I want to review.

Mike: Fine. I've heard that before. But you called the meeting. Fire away.

Ron: Well, Mike, there are several things you need to hear. One is what I noticed during the site tour. I think you're too familiar with some of your female personnel. You know, one of them might take offence and get you involved in a sexual harassment charge.

Mike: Oh, come on. You haven't been around this factory before, and you don't know the informal, friendly relationships we have. The office staff and the women on the floor are flattered by a little attention now and then.

Ron: That may be so, but you need to be more careful. You may not be sensitive to what's really going on with them. And that raises another thing I noticed – the appearance of your shop-floor. You know how important it is in Parker to have a neat and clean shop-floor. As I walked through this morning, I noticed that it wasn't as orderly and neat as I would like to see it. Having things in disarray reflects poorly on you, Mike.

Mike: My site is as neat as any other in Parkers. You may have seen a few tools out of place because someone was just using them, but we take a lot of pride in our neatness. I don't see how you can say that things are in disarray. You've got no experience around here, so who are you to judge?

Ron: Well, I'm glad you're sensitive to the neatness issue. I just think you need to pay attention to it, that's all. But regarding neatness, I notice that you don't dress like a factory manager. I think you're creating a sub-standard impression by not wearing a tie, for example. Such casual dress can be used as an excuse for workers to come to work in really grubby attire. That may not be safe.

Mike: Look, I don't agree with making a big separation between the managers and the employees. By dressing like people out on the shop-floor, I think we eliminate a lot of barriers. Besides, I don't have the money to buy clothes that might get oil on them every day. You seem to be nit-picking.

Ron: I don't want to nit-pick, Mike. But I do feel strongly about the issues I've mentioned. There are some other things, though, that need to get corrected. One is the appearance of the reports you send into head office. There are often mistakes, misspellings, and, I suspect, some wrong numbers. I wonder if you are paying attention to these reports. You seem to be reviewing them superficially.

Mike: If there is one thing we have too much of, it's reports. I could spend three-quarters of my time filling out report forms and generating data for some accountant in head office. We have reports coming out of our ears. Why don't you give us a chance to get our work done and eliminate all this paperwork?

Ron: You know as well as I do, Mike, that we need to carefully monitor our productivity, quality and costs. You just need to be more aware of your responsibility.

Mike: Fine. I'm not going to fight about that. It's a losing battle for me. No one on the top floor will ever reduce their demand for reports. But, listen, Ron, I also have one question for you.

Ron: What's that?

Mike: Why don't you go find somebody else to pick on? I need to get back to work.

Discussion Questions
1. What principles of supportive communication and supportive listening are violated in this case?
2. How could the interaction have been changed to produce a better outcome?
3. Categorise each of the statements by naming the rule of supportive communication that is either illustrated or violated.
4. What should Ron do in his follow-up meeting with Mike?

Rejected Plans

The following dialogue occurred between two employees in a large firm. The conversation illustrates several characteristics of supportive communication.

Helen: How did your meeting go with Mr Peters yesterday?
David: Not so well.
Helen: It looks as if you're pretty upset about it.
David: Yes, I am. It was a totally frustrating experience. Let's just say I would like to forget the whole thing.
Helen: Things can't have gone as well as you had hoped.
David: You can say that again. That man was impossible. I thought the plans I submitted were very clear and well thought out. Then he rejected the entire package.
Helen: You mean he didn't accept any of them?
David: Correct.
Helen: I've seen your work before, David. You've always done a first-rate job. I can't see why your plans were rejected by Mr Peters. What did he say about them?
David: He said they were unrealistic and too difficult to implement, and . . .
Helen: Really?
David: Yes, and then he said that I felt he was attacking me personally. But, on the other hand, I guess I was angry because I thought my plans were very good, and you know, I paid close attention to every detail in those plans.
Helen: I'm certain that you did.
David: It just annoys me.
Helen: I'm sure it does. I would be upset, too.

David: Peters must have something against me.

Helen: After all the effort you put into those plans, you still couldn't work out whether Mr Peters was rejecting you or your plans. Is that right?

David: Yes. How could you tell?

Helen: I can really understand your confusion and uncertainty when you felt Mr Peters' actions were unreasonable.

David: I just don't understand why he did what he did.

Helen: Right. If he said your plans were unrealistic, what does that mean? I mean, how can you deal with a rationale like that? It's just too general – meaningless, even. Did he mention anything specific? Did you ask him to point out some problems or explain the reasons for his rejection more clearly?

David: Good point, but I was so disappointed at the rejection that I just wasn't concentrating. You know what I mean?

Helen: Yes. It's such a demoralising experience. You have so much invested personally that you try to save what little self-respect is left.

David: That's right. I just wanted to get out of there before I said something I would be sorry for.

Helen: Yet, in the back of your mind, you probably thought that Mr Peters wouldn't risk the company's future just because he didn't like you personally. But then, well – the plans were good! It's hard to deal with that contradiction on the spot, isn't it?

David: Exactly. I knew I should have pushed him for more information, but I just stood there like a dummy. But, what can I do about it now? It's spilt milk.

Helen: I don't think it's a total loss, David. I mean, from what you have told me – what he said and what you said – I don't think a conclusion can be reached. Perhaps he doesn't understand the plans, or perhaps it was just his off-day. Who knows, it could be a lot of things. What would you think about pinning Mr Peters down by asking for his objections, point by point? Do you think it would help to talk to him again?

David: Well, I would certainly know a lot more than I know now. As it is, I wouldn't know where to begin revising or modifying the plans. And you're right, I really don't know what Peters thinks about me or my work. Sometimes I just react and interpret with little or no evidence.

Helen: Perhaps another meeting would be a good thing, then.

David: Well, I suppose I'd better get off my high horse and arrange an appointment with him for next week. I am curious to find out what the problem is with the plans, or me. (Pause) Thanks Helen, for helping me sort this out.

Discussion Questions

1. Categorise each statement in the case according to the supportive communication characteristic or type of response it represents. For example, the first statement by David obviously is not very congruent, but the second one is much more so.
2. Which statements in the conversation were most helpful? Which do you think would produce defensiveness or close off the conversation?
3. What are the potential disadvantages of giving outright advice for solving David's problem? Why doesn't Helen just tell David what he ought to do? Is it incongruent to ask David what he thinks is the best solution?

Skill Practice

Exercises for Diagnosing Problems and Fostering Understanding

Vulcan Computers

Background

The role of manager encompasses not only one-to-one coaching and counselling with an employee, but it also frequently entails helping other people understand coaching and counselling principles for themselves. Sometimes it means refereeing interactions and, by example, helping other people learn about correct principles of supportive communication. This is part of the task in this exercise. In a group setting, coaching and counselling become more difficult because multiple messages, driven by multiple motives, all interact. Skilled supportive communicators, however, help each group member feel supported and understood in the interaction, even though the solution to the issue is not always the one he or she would have preferred.

Assignment

In this exercise you should apply the principles of supportive communication. First, form into groups of four people each. Next, read the case and assign the following roles in your group: Mike, Sheila, John and an observer. Assume that a meeting is being held with Mike, Sheila and John immediately after the end of the incidents in the following case. Play the roles you have been assigned and try to resolve the problems. The observer should provide feedback to the three players at the end of the exercise. (An Observer's Form to assist the observer in providing feedback can be found in the Scoring Key at the end of the book, page 74.)

The Case

Vulcan Computers is a medium-sized computer hardware manufacturer based in the South East of England. The parts are part-made in Taiwan and finished and assembled in the English factory, which is also the company's research and engineering centre.

The process design group consists of eight male engineers and their supervisor, Mike Coombes. They have worked well together for a number of years, and good relationships have developed among all the members. When the workload began to increase, Mike recruited a new design engineer, Sheila Williams, who recently received a first class honours degree in engineering at Durham University. Her first assignment is to join a project team which is working on Vulcan's computer notebook. The three other members of the team are John Smith (aged 38, 15 years with the company), Philip Jones (aged 40, ten years with the company) and Kevin Robson (aged 32, eight years with the company).

As a new Vulcan employee, Sheila is fired with enthusiasm. She finds the work challenging as it offers her the opportunity to apply much of the knowledge she has gained at University. Although she is friendly with the rest of the project team, Sheila doesn't socialise much with them at work and doesn't join them for their traditional Friday night get-together at the Red Lion.

Sheila takes her work seriously and she regularly works after hours. Because of her persistence, coupled with her more recent education, she regularly finishes her portion of the various project stages several days ahead of her colleagues. She finds this irritating as it means she is constantly having to ask Mike Coombes for additional work to keep her busy until the rest of the team has caught up with her. Initially she offered to help John, Philip and Kevin with their assignments, but each time she was abruptly turned down.

About five months after Sheila had joined the design group, John asked to see Mike about a problem the group was having. Their conversation went as follows:

Mike: What's the problem, John?
John: Look Mike, I don't want to waste your time, but some of the

other design engineers want me to discuss Sheila with you. She is irritating everyone with her know-it-all, pompous attitude. She's just not the kind of person we want to work with.

Mike: I can't understand that, John. She's an excellent worker, and her design work is always well done and usually flawless. She's doing everything the company wants her to do.

John: The company never asked her to disrupt the morale of the group or to tell us how to do our work. The animosity in our group could eventually result in lower-quality work from the whole unit.

Mike: I'll tell you what I'll do. Sheila has a meeting with me next week to discuss her six-month performance. I'll keep your thoughts in mind, but I can't promise an improvement in what you and the others believe is a pompous attitude.

John: Immediate improvement in her behaviour is not the problem, it's her coaching others when she has no right to. She publicly shows others what to do. You'd think she was lecturing an advanced class in design with all her high-powered, useless equations and formulas. If she keeps this up there's going to be some real trouble.

Mike couldn't ignore John's views. A week later he called Sheila into his office for her first six-month review. Part of the conversation went as follows:

Mike: There is one other aspect I'd like to discuss with you. As I've explained there's no problem with your technical performance but there are some questions about your relationships with the other workers.

Sheila: I don't understand – what questions are you talking about?

Mike: Well, to be quite frank, certain members of the design group have complained about your apparent know-it-all-attitude and the manner in which you try to tell them how to do their jobs. You're going to have to be patient with them and not publicly call them out about their performance. This is a good group of engineers, and their work over the years has been more than acceptable. I don't want any problems that will cause the group to produce less effectively.

Sheila: Let me make a few comments. First of all, I have never publicly criticised their performance to them or to you. Initially, when I finished ahead of them, I offered to help them with their work but was bluntly told to mind my own business. I took the hint and concentrated only on my part of the work. What you don't understand is that after five months of working in this group I have come to the conclusion that these engineers are working as slowly as they possibly can – they're ripping off the company. They're setting a work pace much slower than they're capable of. They're more interested in the music from Sam's radio, the local soccer team and going to the Red Lion. I'm sorry, but this is just not the way I was brought up or trained. And finally, they've never looked on me as a qualified engineer, but as a woman who has broken their professional barrier.

Revised from a case-study by A.D. Szilagyi and M.J.Wallace, (1983) from Organizational Behaviour and Performance, 3rd ed. (Glenview, Ill.: Foresman and Co.,1983, pp 204 – 205).

Brown vs. Thomas

Background

Effective one-to-one coaching and counselling are skills that are required in many settings in life, not just in management. It is hard to imagine anyone who would not benefit from training in supportive communication. Because there are so many aspects of supportive communication, however, it is sometimes difficult to remember all of them. That is why practice, with observation and feedback, is so important. These attributes of supportive communication can become a natural part of your interaction approach as you conscientiously practise and receive feedback from a colleague.

Assignment

In the following exercise, one individual should study the role of Harriet Brown, another the role of Judy Thomas. To make the role-play realistic, do not read each other's role descriptions. When you have finished reading, role-play a meeting between Harriet Brown and Judy Thomas. A third person should serve as the observer. (An Observer's Form to assist the observer in providing feedback can be found in the Scoring Key at the end of the book, page 74.)

Harriet Brown, Department Head

You are Harriet Brown, head of a bank's operations department. You have only been in the organisation for two years and have been quickly promoted. You enjoy working for this bank. It has a high reputation and is acknowledged for its commitment to management development and training programmes. External courses are paid for by the bank and each employee is given an opportunity for a personal management interview each month and these sessions are usually extremely productive.

One of the department members, Judy Thomas, has been in this department for 19 years, 15 of them in the same job. She is reasonably good at what she does, and she is always punctual and efficient. She tends to get to work earlier than most employees in order to read the *Financial Times* and trade magazines. You can almost set your watch by the time Judy has her coffee breaks and by the time she phones her daughter every afternoon.

Your view is that although Judy is a good worker, she lacks imagination and initiative. This has been indicated by her lack of merit increases over the last five years and by the fact that she has had the same job for 15 years. She's content to do just what is assigned, nothing more. Your predecessor must have given hints to Judy that she might be in line for a promotion, however, because Judy has raised this with you more than once. Because she has been in her job so long, she is at the top of her pay range, and without a promotion, she cannot receive a salary adjustment above the basic cost-of-living increase.

The one thing Judy does beyond the basic minimum job requirements is to help train young people who come into the department. She is very patient and methodical with them, and she seems to take pride in helping them learn. She has not been hesitant to point out this contribution to you. Unfortunately, this activity does not qualify Judy for a promotion, nor could she be transferred into the training and development department. Once you suggested that she take a few courses at the local college, paid for by the bank, but she simply said that she was too old to go back to school. You think that she might be intimidated because she didn't go to college.

As much as you would like to promote Judy, there just doesn't seem to be any way to do that in good conscience. You have tried putting additional work under her control, but she seems to be slowing down in her productivity rather than speeding up. The work needs to be done, and expanding her role just puts you behind schedule.

This impending interview is probably your best chance to talk openly with Judy about her performance and her potential. You certainly don't want to lose her as an employee, but there is not going to be a change in job assignment for a long time unless she changes her performance dramatically.

Judy Thomas, Department Member

You are a member of a bank's operations department. You have been with the bank for 19 years, 15 of them in the same job. You enjoy working for the bank because of its friendly atmosphere, and the job is fairly secure. However, lately you have become more dissatisfied as you've seen person after person come into the bank and get promoted ahead of you. Your own boss, Harriet Brown, is almost 20 years your junior. Another woman who joined the bank at the same time as you is now a senior manager at head office. You can't understand why you've been neglected. You are efficient and accurate in your work, you have a near-perfect attendance record and you consider yourself to be a good employee. You have gone out of your way on many occasions to help train and orient young people who are just joining the bank. Several of them have written letters later telling you how important your help was in getting them promoted. A lot of good that does you!

The only explanation you can think of is that there is a bias against you because you haven't been to college or university. On the other hand, others have moved up without a degree. You haven't taken advantage of any college courses paid for by the bank. The last thing you want after a long day's work is another three hours in a lecture room. Anyway, you only see your family in the evenings, and you don't want to take time away from them. It doesn't take a college degree to do your job anyway.

Your monthly personal management interview is coming up with your department head, Harriet Brown, and you've decided the time has come to get a few answers. Several things need explaining. Not only have you not been promoted, but you haven't even received a merit increase for five years. You're not getting any credit for the extra contributions you make with new employees, nor for your steady, reliable work. Could anyone blame you for being a little bitter?

Skill Application

Application Activities for Communicating Supportively

Suggested Further Assignments

1. Tape-record an interview with someone such as a co-worker, friend or spouse. Focus on the issues or challenges faced right now by that other person. Try to assume the role of coach or counsellor. Categorise your statements in the interview on the basis of the supportive communication principles in this book. (The Rejected Plans case, detailed previously provides an example of such an interview.)

2. Teach someone you know the concepts of supportive communication and supportive listening. Provide your own explanations and illustrations so the person understands what you are talking about. Describe your experience in your work book.

3. Think of an interpersonal problem you share with someone, such as a flatmate, parent, friend or instructor. Discuss the problem with that person, using supportive communication. Write about the experience in as much detail as possible. Concentrate on the extent to which you and the other person used the eight principles of supportive communication. Record and describe areas in which you need to improve.

4. Write two mini case studies. One should recount an effective coaching or counselling situation. The other should recount an ineffective coaching or counselling situation. The cases should be based on a real event either in your own personal experience or in the experience of someone you know well. Use all the principles of supportive communication and listening in your cases.

Application Plan and Evaluation

The intent of this exercise is to help you apply your skills in a real-life, out-of-class setting. Now that you have become familiar with the behavioural guidelines that form the basis of effective skill performance, you will improve more by trying out those guidelines in an everyday context. The trouble is, unlike a classroom activity in which feedback is immediate and others can assist you with their evaluations, this skill application activity is one you must accomplish and evaluate on your own. There are two parts to this activity. Part 1 helps prepare you to apply the skill. Part 2 helps you evaluate and improve on your experience. Be sure to actually write down answers to each item. Don't short-circuit the process by skipping steps.

Part 1 – Planning
1. Write down the two or three aspects of this skill that are most important to you. These may be areas of weakness, areas you most want to improve or areas that are most salient to a problem you face currently. Identify the specific aspects of this skill that you want to apply.
2. Now identify the setting or the situation in which you will apply this skill. Establish a plan for performance by actually writing down the situation. Who else will be involved? When will you do it? Where will it be done?
3. Identify the specific behaviours you will engage in to apply this skill. Operationalise your skill performance.
4. What are the indicators of successful performance? How will you know you have succeeded in being effective? What will indicate that you have performed competently?

Part 2 – Evaluation
5. After you have completed your implementation, record the results. What happened? How successful were you? What was the effect on others?
6. How can you improve? What modifications can you make next time? What will you do differently in a similar situation in the future?
7. Looking back on your whole skill practice and application experience, what have you learned? What has been surprising? In what ways might this experience help you in the long term?

Scoring Key

Communicating Supportively

Skill area	Items	Assessment pre-	post-
Knowledge of coaching and counselling	1, 2, 20	————	————
Providing effective negative feedback	3, 4, 5, 6, 7, 8	————	————
Communicating supportively	9, 10, 11, 12, 13, 14, 15, 16, 17, 18, 19	————	————
TOTAL SCORE		————	————

To assess how well you scored on this instrument, compare your scores to three comparison standards:

- Compare your scores against the maximum possible (120).
- Compare your scores with the scores of other students in your class.
- Compare your scores to a norm group consisting of 500 business school students. In comparison to the norm group, if you scored:

> 99 or above, you are in the top quartile;
> 93 to 98, you are in the second quartile;
> 87 to 92, you are in the third quartile;
> 86 or below, you are in the bottom quartile.

Communicating Styles

Part I: Identify the type of response pattern that you rely on most when required to be a coach or a counsellor by adding the numbers you gave to the response alternatives in Part 1. For example, if in question one you chose a) as your first choice, then list 1a) below as 3; if your second response choice was c) list 1c) below as 2; finally if your last response choice was e) list 1e) below as 1. Repeat this for all the questions and then total the scores for questions 1–4 for each response type.

The most skilled supportive communicators score 9 or above on Reflecting responses and 6 or more on Probing responses. They score 2 or less on Advising responses and 4 or less on Deflecting responses.

The chapter discusses the advantages and disadvantages of each of these response types.

1. a. Deflecting response ——
   b. Probing response ——
   c. Advising response ——
   d. Reflecting response ——
   e. Deflecting response ——
2. a. Reflecting response ——
   b. Deflecting response ——
   c. Advising response ——
   d. Reflecting response ——
   e. Probing response ——
3. a. Probing response ——
   b. Deflecting response ——
   c. Advising response ——
   d. Reflecting response ——
   e. Probing response ——
4. a. Reflecting response ——
   b. Probing response ——
   c. Deflecting response ——
   d. Deflecting response ——
   e. Advising response ——

Part II: Circle the alternative that you chose. The most skilled communicators select alternatives 1a, 2d, 3e, 4h, and 5i.

1. a. Problem-oriented statement
   b. Person-oriented statement
2. c. Incongruent/minimising statement
   d. Congruent statement
3. e. Descriptive statement
   f. Evaluative statement
4. g. Invalidating statement
   h. Validating statement
5. i. Owned statement
   j. Disowned statement

Observer's Feedback Form

Diagnosing Problems and Fostering Understanding

Vulcan Computers/ Brown vs. Thomas

As the observer, rate the extent to which the role-players performed the following behaviours effectively. Place the initials of each individual beside the number on the scale that best represents performance. Identify specific things that each person can do to improve his or her performance.

ACTION	RATING (1=low, 5=high)
1. Used problem-oriented communication.	_____
2. Communicated congruently.	_____
3. Used descriptive communication.	_____
4. Used validating communication.	_____
5. Used specific and qualified communication.	_____
6. Used conjunctive communication.	_____
7. Owned statements and used personal words.	_____
8. Listened attentively.	_____
9. Used a variety of response alternatives.	_____

Comments:

Glossary

Clarification probe	A request to make a statement more clear – 'Can you clarify what you have just said, I am not quite clear what you mean?'
Coaching	A term used for the process whereby managers assist their subordinates to perform their work by setting standards, providing training and support, and giving advice.
Communication	In the context of this book, communication is about the process of human interaction and not about the tools we may or may not use – the process by which individuals and groups influence each other.
Congruence	Matching one's own behaviour to what the other person is thinking or feeling – at its simplest, congruence is established by deciding the right place, time and context for communication.
Consulting	Once a subordinate has been allowed to develop his or her own work style to face a particular issue, then he or she is certainly in possession of more local and 'expert' information on what the task entails. In supportive communication this is acknowledged by the manager and the subordinate's expertise is recognised – he or she is consulted when the work is being discussed.
Counselling	In the management context counselling is not associated with the psychiatrist's chair, but with frank one-to-one interviews where managers and subordinates discuss the personal issues faced in performing work effectively. Counselling is not about giving advice or direction but facing individual work-related issues.
Descriptive communication	Communication involving an objective account of the event or behaviour that is a cause of your concern, developing the reaction or consequences of the event or behaviour and how it makes you feel, and suggestions for more acceptable alternatives while giving support to the individual concerned.
Diagnostic surveys	In the world of psychology there is a clear distinction between questionnaires and tests. Tests have validity; they can be replicated and used to compare between individuals and they have what we may call a provenance which may be checked by those who use them. Questionnaires are much

less formal, and although useful, cannot be relied upon for comparisons between individuals and groups. Diagnostic surveys, as used in this book, are intended to assist individuals to gain an insight into their own behaviour, beliefs and capabilities.

Directive communication

One-way communication where a dominant party gives instructions or orders without concern of the feelings of others.

Egalitarian communication

Communication which accepts that, on a particular issue, each has an equal claim to a valid opinion.

Elaboration probe

A request for more detail in a discussion – 'Can you elaborate on what you have just said?'

Imperviousness

A barrier that excludes any argument or discussion from others.

Invalidating communication

Communication that denies not only the right for others to have opinions but also, in the extreme, the right of the individual to be worth consideration.

Reflection probe

A method of getting further information by repeating the sense, if not the exact words, of the person being questioned – 'You say you were made to feel inferior by his response. How was that?'

Repetition probe

A return to a previous subject when the item has not been cleared up – 'Once again I must press the point, what did you actually do?'

Shadow

In the psychology of Jung, the shadow of an individual is considered as their 'dark side'. Here we take the word in a more metaphorical sense as being something that is outside our control.

Skills

The word 'skill' has a very definite meaning in management development. Three classifications – knowledge, skills and aptitude – need to be utilised to perform any effective task. We need to know what has to be done, how it is to be done – skills; and have the ability and willingness to do it – aptitude.

Supportive communication

Communication between managers and their subordinates that is effective in assisting the achievement of the task and allows each party top feel valued.

Theory X and theory Y

The concept is that managers have two polarities of their views on the reasons why the people around them work. If they follow Theory X they see people who need to be MADE to work, as opposed to those who follow Theory Y who accept that people may have bad days, but on the whole, given the right tools and conditions, actually like working. Theory Z, also proposed by McGregor and developed later by others, allows us some middle ground – a view between X and Y.

Validating communication

Communication that confirms the value of the individual as a human being, regardless of influence finally granted to his or her views.

World class

As a global market takes hold, organisations find that being a good company within their own national boundaries is not enough. They have to compare themselves – be benchmarked – against ALL the companies world-wide.

References

Athos, A. & Gabarro, J. *Interpersonal behavior*. Englewood Cliffs, N.J.: Prentice-Hall, 1978.

Barnlund, D. C. *Interpersonal communication: Survey and studies*. Boston: Houghton Mifflin, 1968.

Benjamin, A. *The helping interview*. Boston: Houghton Mifflin, 1969.

Blanchard, K.H. & Johnson, S. *The one minute manager*. London: Fontana, 1983.

Boss, Wayne L. Team building and the problem of regression: The personal management interview as an intervention. *Journal of Applied Behavioral Science*, 1983, 19, 67-83.

Cameron, Kim. *Organizational downsizing and large-scale change*. Working paper, The University of Michigan, 1988.

Crocker, J. *Speech communication instruction based on employers' perceptions of the importance of selected communication skills for employees on the job*. Paper presented at the Speech Communication Association meeting, Minneapolis, Minn., 1978.

Dyer, W.G. *Congruence. In the sensitive manipulator*. Provo, Utah: Brigham Young University Press, 1972.

Galbraith, J. K. Are you Mark Epernay? The literary Galbraith on the art of writing. *Christian Science Monitor*, December 9, 1975, p. 19.

Gibb, J. R. Defensive communication. *Journal of Communication*, 1961, 11, 141-148.

Glasser, W. *Reality therapy: A new approach to psychiatry*. New York: Harper & Row, 1965.

Goffman, E. On face-work: An analysis of ritual elements in social interaction. *Psychiatry*, 1955, 18, 213-231.

Haney, W. V. *Communication and interpersonal relations*. Homewood, Ill.: Irwin, 1979.

Hanson, Gary. *Determinants of firm performance: An integration of economic and organizational factors*. Unpublished doctoral dissertation, University of Michigan Business School, 1986.

Hersey, P. & Blanchard, K.H. *Management of Organisational Behaviour*. New Jersey: Prentice-Hall, 1969.

Huseman, R. C., Lahiff, J. M. & Hatfield, J. D. *Interpersonal communication in organizations*. Boston: Holbrook Press, 1976.

Jacobs, M. *Levels of confirmation and disconfirmation in interpersonal communications*. Unpublished doctoral dissertation. University of Denver, 1973.

James, W. Cited in R. D. Laing, Mystification, confusion, and conflict. In I. Boszormenya-Nagy, J. L. Framo (Eds.), *Intensive family therapy*. New York: Harper & Row, 1965.

Loomis, F. *The consultation room*. New York: Knopf, 1939.

Maier, N. R. F., Solem, A. R. & Maier, A. A. Counselling, interviewing, and job contacts. In N. R. F. Maier (Ed.), *Psychology of industrial organizations*. Boston: Houghton Mifflin, 1973.

McGregor, Douglas. *The human side of enterprise*. New York: McGraw-Hill, 1960.

Ouchi, William. *Theory Z*. Reading, Mass.: Addison-Wesley, 1981.

Peters, Tom. *Thriving on chaos*. New York: Knopf, 1988.

Rogers, C. W. *On becoming a person*. Boston: Houghton Mifflin, 1961.

Rogers, C. & Farson, R. *Active Listening*. Chicago: Industrial Relations Center, 1976.

Ross, David. *Coaching and counselling*. Unpublished manuscript, University of Michigan Executive Education Center, 1986.

Sieburg, E. *Dysfunctional communication and interpersonal responsiveness in small groups*. Unpublished doctoral dissertation, University of Denver, 1969.

Sieburg, E. *Confirming and disconfirming organizational communication*. Working paper, University of Denver, 1978.

Steil, L. K. *Your listening profile*. Minneapolis: Sperry Corporation, 1980.

Thorton, B. B. As you were saying – The number one problem. *Personnel Journal*, 1966, 45, 237-238

Woods, Mike and Whitehead, Jackie. *Working alone*. London: Pitman, 1993.

Index